Peloponnesian War 431–404 BC

COMBAT
Athenian Hoplite
VERSUS
Spartan Hoplite

Murray Dahm

Illustrated by Adam Hook

OSPREY PUBLISHING

Bloomsbury Publishing Plc

Kemp House, Chawley Park, Cumnor Hill, Oxford OX2 9PH, UK

1385 Broadway, 5th Floor, New York, NY 10018, USA

E-mail: info@ospreypublishing.com

www.ospreypublishing.com

OSPREY is a trademark of Osprey Publishing Ltd

First published in Great Britain in 2021

A catalogue record for this book is available from the British Library.

ISBN: PB 9781472844125; eBook 9781472844132;
ePDF 9781472844101; XML 9781472844118

21 22 23 24 25   10 9 8 7 6 5 4 3 2 1

Maps by www.bounford.com
Index by Rob Munro
Typeset by PDQ Digital Media Solutions, Bungay, UK
Printed and bound in India by Replika Press Private Ltd.

Osprey Publishing supports the Woodland Trust, the UK's leading woodland conservation charity.

To find out more about our authors and books visit **www.ospreypublishing.com**. Here you will find extracts, author interviews, details of forthcoming events and the option to sign up for our newsletter.

Artist's note

Readers may care to note that the original paintings from which the colour plates in this book were prepared are available for private sale. All reproduction copyright whatsoever is retained by the publishers. All enquiries should be addressed to:

scorpiopaintings@btinternet.com

The publishers regret that they can enter into no correspondence upon this matter.

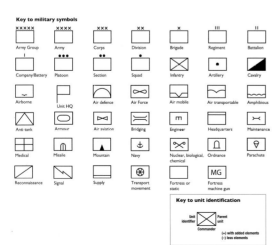

CONTENTS

Introduction

The seeds of the Peloponnesian War (431–404 BC), fought between the city-states of Sparta and Athens and their respective allies, were sown some 50 years earlier through the successes of the Greek states in defeating the second Persian invasion of Greece (480–479 BC). Eleven years previously, at the culmination of the first Persian invasion of Greece (490 BC), Athens stood alone at the battle of Marathon; this unexpected Athenian victory encouraged the city-state to see itself as Sparta's equal. Sparta had always been considered to be the 'natural' leader of Greece because of its unique political system which meant Spartan citizens trained in warfare full time. Other Greek city-states had citizen soldiers with minimal training who were called out as needed.

In 480 BC, a second Persian invasion saw Athens and Sparta lead the defence of Greece at the battle of Thermopylae and the naval battle of Artemisium (fought simultaneously in August or September 480 BC), the battle of Salamis (September 480 BC) and the battles of Plataea and Mycale (August 479 BC). These victories created and fostered a self-confidence in the Greek states which led to an inevitable power struggle between Sparta and Athens. Even the ancients recognized that Sparta, boasting a formidable army and a political system designed to produce the best hoplites, was the natural leader of the Greeks on land. At the same time, Athens was recognized as the dominant sea power, having furnished the largest number of ships during the Greco-Persian Wars (499–449 BC) and continuing to have the most powerful navy (Thucydides 4.12.3).

Following the Persian Wars, Sparta continued to dominate land-based Greek cities that lacked sea power – and those which had navies but were threatened by Athens – and, through the Peloponnesian League, established a powerful network of allies throughout Greece. At the same time, however, Sparta was a conservative and traditional culture and did not embrace the idea of empire building, especially not when it involved

overseas territories. By contrast, Athens took every opportunity to build a sea-based empire. Athens assumed the leadership of the Delian League, a naval alliance intended to keep Persian influence at bay, then systematically turned the Delian League into an empire. The five decades following the Persian Wars (literally the 'fifty-year period' – the *pentecontaetia*) saw Athens and Sparta come into inevitable conflict as their allies, spheres of influence and even the contrasting cultures of the two city-states collided with one another.

The first steps towards this inevitable conflict came when Athens' dominance of the Delian League caused the Spartans to become alarmed at the growth of Athenian power. Beginning in 461 BC, Athens built a series of protective walls between the city and the harbours of the Piraeus and the Phalerum that appeared to be preparations for a bigger war. The walls meant Athens could maintain access to its harbours even if the city was under siege. An intermittent series of conflicts occurred, which are now known as the First Peloponnesian War (460–445 BC), but these ended with the Thirty Years' Peace of 445 BC by which Athens and Sparta agreed to recognize each other's sphere of influence and also to guarantee any other state's right to join either side or to remain neutral. The ideas of 'spheres of influence' and a 'right to neutrality' are important in developing an understanding of how war broke out again in 431 BC. The city-state of Corinth was an ally of Sparta, but several Corinthian colonies were dominated by Athens (Corcyra at its own request and Potidaea forcibly). Corinth understandably agitated for Spartan intervention against Athenian activities. The city of Megara, also an ally of Sparta, was then forbidden to trade with Athens or its allies. Then the city of Thebes, another ally

When the Peloponnesian War began, almost the entire Greek world was allied with Sparta or with Athens. These alliances stretched from Magna Graecia in the west to the coast of Asia Minor in the east. Sparta began the war limited by where the Spartans could march their armies; the Spartan navy was small and unskilled. Sparta therefore marched to invade Attica each year, and sent armies to create trouble for Athens or its allies such as Heracleia. Athens, by contrast, was constrained only by where it could reach with the Athenian fleet. Thus, the Athenians were able to engage in campaigns in the Aegean, as far north as Potidaea and Amphipolis, and also harass the Peloponnesian coast and the islands of Corcyra and Zacynthus, and even intervene on Sicily. Athens therefore chose to split its forces into several smaller fleets with limited numbers of men and, at home, defended the long walls of Athens.

of Sparta, attacked the city of Plataea, one of Athens' allies. All of these actions foreshadowed a larger war and in 431 BC, the Spartans and their allies decided that Athens had broken the terms of the peace treaty of 445 BC. Spartan and allied forces duly invaded Athens' home territory of Attica and ravaged the land, destroying crops and farms.

The pre-eminent political leader in Athens at the outbreak of war was Pericles, son of the politician and general Xanthippus. Pericles had foreseen that these seasonal invasions would be the Spartan tactic and, rather than face the Spartans on land, he suggested a policy whereby the population of Attica would withdraw into safety behind the walls around Athens and the Piraeus, survive on maritime trade, and avoid facing the Spartans in the land battles the invaders were trying to provoke. The Athenians' intention was to launch naval raids into Peloponnesian territory from the safety of their walled harbours. The Athenians followed this approach for the first years of the war despite the unpopularity of allowing their farms and homes to be destroyed. Pericles survived a challenge to his primacy and the policy continued. The Spartan invasions were an annual event, but were only temporary as Spartan forces returned home after they had destroyed the Athenians' crops and farms. It is difficult to assess how much damage these invasions caused, but they cannot have destroyed all of the Athenian harvest or reached every corner of Attica. Also, it must have been frustrating for the Spartans to know that their mighty army had been reduced to burning crops and farms.

Behind the walls of Athens, however, with the population of the countryside crammed into a small space for shelter, plague broke out in 430/429 BC and again in 427/426 BC. Disastrously for Athens, Pericles himself died of the plague in 429 BC. Thereafter Athens was beset with another kind of plague – demagogues whose words whipped the Athenian voters into a frenzy and who sought only political power but had no clear policy for winning the war; such men became more and more prominent in Athenian politics. Two parties dominated – one led by Nicias (who favoured defence) and the other by Cleon (who favoured aggression). When Cleon died at the battle of Amphipolis in 422 BC, there were many more aspiring demagogues waiting to take his place. Their ambitions would prove disastrous for Athens.

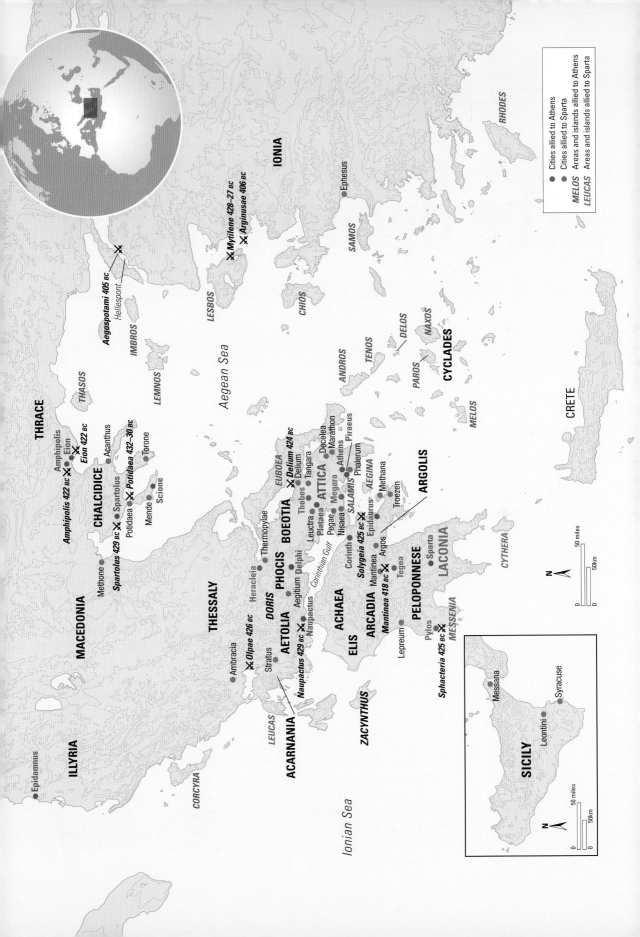

THRACE

Amphipolis
Amphipolis 422 BC ✗✗
Eïon
Eïon 422 BC
Acanthus

MACEDONIA

CHALCIDICE

Methone
Spartolus 429 BC ✗✗ Spartolus
Potidaea ✗✗ *Potidaea 432–30 BC*
Mende
Torone
Scione

THASOS

ILLYRIA

Epidamnus

Aegospotami 405 BC ✗✗
Hellespont

IMBROS

LEMNOS

✗✗ *Mytilene 428–27 BC*
✗✗ *Arginusae 406 BC*

LESBOS

IONIA

Ephesus

CHIOS

SAMOS

RHODES

Aegean Sea

DELOS

NAXOS
PAROS

TENOS
ANDROS

CYCLADES

MELOS

CRETE

THESSALY

Ambracia
Stratus

ACARNANIA

LEUCAS

CORCYRA

Ionian Sea

ZACYNTHUS

✗✗ *Olpae 426 BC*
Heracleia
Thermopylae

DORIS

Delphi
Aegitium
Naupactus 429 BC ✗✗ Naupactus

AETOLIA

PHOCIS

EUBOEA

✗✗ *Delium 424 BC*
Delium
Thebes
Tangara
Plataea
Leuctra

BOEOTIA

Decelea
Marathon
Athens
Piraeus
Phalerum

ATTICA

Megara
Pegae
Nisaea

SALAMIS

AEGINA

Methana
Troezen

Corinthian Gulf
Corinth

ACHAEA

ELIS

Lepreum

Pylos
Sphacteria 425 BC ✗✗

MESSENIA

ARCADIA

Mantinea
Mantinea 418 BC ✗✗
Tegea

Solygeia 425 BC ✗✗
Epidaurus
Argos

ARGOLIS

PELOPONNESE

Sparta

LACONIA

CYTHERA

50 miles
50km

N

SICILY

Messana
Leontini
Syracuse

50 miles
50km

N

• Cities allied to Athens
• Cities allied to Sparta
MELOS Areas and islands allied to Athens
LEUCAS Areas and islands allied to Sparta

The Opposing Sides

EQUIPMENT AND TACTICS

One of the most remarkable aspects of the Peloponnesian War is that both sides – Athens and Sparta and their respective allies – fought on land in essentially the same manner. In a reflection of their shared cultural values, the city-states of Greece had adopted hoplite warfare in about the 7th century BC. The nature and precise date of the adoption of hoplite warfare are still matters of controversy, but the iconography of the hoplite from pottery, sculpture and literature reveals a great deal.

The hoplite (*hoplites* in Greek) was the heavy infantryman in Greek armies from the 7th century to the 4th century BC. Sparta was the undisputed master of hoplite warfare, dedicating the whole of its adult male citizenry to the art of the hoplite and full-time training for war. Athens had more citizens than Sparta, but they served as soldiers only when required and so were understandably regarded as being inferior, as were the populations of the other Greek cities.

Primarily armed with a spear (*dory*) and carrying a shield (*aspis*), the hoplite represented the pinnacle of Greek manly military virtue across a multitude of states which all invested heavily in the hoplite phalanx. The nature of the hoplite phalanx remains controversial but it was a formation of heavy infantry who engaged in combat in close formation with the enemy phalanx. Every hoplite also carried a sword, the straight *xiphos* or the curved *machaira* or *kopis* or, at Sparta, the short *encheiridion*. Other hoplite equipment included a helmet (*kranos*) in a variety of styles and body armour in the form of the cuirass (*spolades*), known today as the *linothorax*; it was usually made of linen although bronze 'muscled' cuirasses are also depicted on sculpture and pottery. As the war progressed, surviving evidence suggests that the hoplite wore little more than his cloak, issued to both Spartan and Athenian recruits. The evidence also suggests the use of *pilos* helmets, which were cheaper and

quicker to produce than Corinthian or Illyrian helmets, although these earlier types continued in use.

Men were provided with shields by the state when they completed their hoplite training. Contemporary art shows that shield decoration could still be as varied as in earlier ages. Shield devices (*episema*) could be appliqué bronze blazons or painted (Plutarch, *Moralia* 234C–D/*Sayings of Spartans Anonymous* 41). There is evidence, however, both in art and literature, that Greek cities started applying capital letters to their shields. A fragment of a play by the Athenian Eupolis, a contemporary of Aristophanes (fragment 394), offers the best evidence available of a capital lambda (Λ; the 11th letter of the Greek alphabet) being used as a Spartan shield device during the Peloponnesian War. A later passage from Xenophon (*Hellenica* 4.4.10) notes that the Sikyonians had a capital sigma (Σ; the 18th letter of the Greek alphabet) on their shields. Pottery of the era depicts many other letter blazons being used, however, although no example depicting a lambda survives. Later, in the 360s BC (*Hellenica* 7.5.20), the Thebans put Heracles' club on their shields, but this too may have occurred earlier.

During the Peloponnesian War, the Athenians sought to avoid open hoplite conflict with any significant Spartan force, knowing that Athens' own strength lay in its navy, the Spartan fleet being much smaller and less experienced than the Athenian fleet. The Greek states' emphasis on hoplite warfare belied the fact that, for the most part, the topography of Greece simply did not feature the flat terrain necessary for such heavy-infantry combat. Sparta and Athens also fielded hoplites from other cities – both made use of allied forces – and Sparta could also call upon the *perioeci* ('dwellers around'), inhabitants of the regions of Laconia and the Peloponnese who were not Spartan citizens. Battlefields in Greece often saw more than one battle fought on them, and the plain-filled region of Boeotia was known as 'the dancing floor of war' (Plutarch, *Moralia* 193E/*Sayings of Kings and Commanders* 18).

Other troop-types were also commonly used by both sides, such as archers (*toxotai*) and lightly armed troops, generically called *psiloi* in Athens

although there are also references to javelinmen (*akontistai*), slingers (*sphendonetai*) and peltasts, lightly armed troops who carried the smaller *pelte* shield. There were also cavalry (*hippeis*) although their numbers were limited – even Athens, the largest Greek city-state, had only 1,200 cavalry. The advantages of recruiting from places such as Thessaly for cavalry and Thrace for lightly armed troops and peltasts were beginning to be recognized in this period. In many battle accounts, however, it is the numbers of hoplites alone which are recorded and emphasized.

The nature of hoplite combat is also fiercely debated. This was the *othismos* or 'push', in which lines of heavily armed hoplites with overlapping shields crashed into each other in an effort to push the opposing line off the battlefield. Traditionally, scholars of hoplite warfare understood this form of combat to be a literal shoving match, comparing it to a rugby scrum. Various commentators, however, have challenged this interpretation, arguing in favour of a more figurative model in which there was not so much pushing as jostling for position and much more weapon play – in the press of a literal *othismos* there can have been little room to manoeuvre weapons, or men for that matter. Indeed, many hoplite battles seem to be very straightforward affairs, with hoplite lines coming up against one another.

Found in Eretria, Greece, and now in the National Archaeological Museum, Athens, this white-ground *lekythos* (oil jug) depicts a young warrior. It dates from 450–440 BC and is attributed to the Achilles Painter. (De Agostini/Getty Images)

The accounts of the three battles examined in this book adhere to a literal model of the *othismos*. In the present author's view, it requires a deliberate misreading of the sources to argue that hoplites did not try to get into close combat with one another and drive the opponent from the field. The increasing depth of the hoplite phalanx across the period argues for this too. At the same time, however, in the three battles examined there is evidence of tactical innovations in hoplite warfare – outflanking manoeuvres, envelopment and the use of lightly armed troops as well as reserves and ambushes – which demand a more nuanced interpretation of exactly what occurred in hoplite combat.

Although the two fighting styles and the equipment employed by Athenian and Spartan hoplites did not differ greatly from one another – all hoplites usually fought in a particular way – it was recognized that because the entire adult male population of Sparta trained full time, the Spartans were simply better at hoplite warfare. Other city-states such as Argos, Elis, Boeotia and even Athens itself had elite forces which were paid by the state to train full time, but these were usually much smaller units, sometimes only 300 men strong. Athens had by this time begun to pay its rowers, hoplites, cavalry and archers, although this may only have been when they were actively campaigning.

Much of the classical hoplite equipment continued to be employed during the Peloponnesian War. The Corinthian helmet remained in use, as did the *aspis* (the interior workings of which are shown beautifully here). The *dory* and sword also continued to be used. Greaves fell out of use before the Peloponnesian War; armour became simpler and the cloak became more common (and was viewed as a symbol of rank in both Athens and Sparta). (Jona Lendering/Wikimedia/CC0)

It is possible to get some idea of ancient hoplite drill, although it can only be glimpsed at: the three battles examined in this book feature wheelings, close order (*pyknosis*) and locked shields (*synaspismos*), and there is later evidence of counter-marches – even the 'Spartan' or 'Laconian' counter-march, which saw troops face the rear but always with the best men in the front rank (Xenophon, *Spartan Constitution* 10.8). In general, however, when a writer describes hoplites in action, it seems to be assumed that the reader will know what that means and how it looked. What is more, precise detail of battle tactics is not usually given in historical narratives. Much of the drill is implied in later manuals termed *Tactica*, written from the 3rd century BC onwards to describe the Macedonian and Hellenistic phalanx (although the earliest surviving example, that of Asclepiodotus, dates from the 1st century BC). In these are descriptions of manoeuvres which were probably also used in hoplite phalanxes. Orders for a turn – *epistrophe* for a 'quarter-turn' or *perispasmos* for a 'half-turn' (Aelian, *Tactica* 24.2) – must have been the same in a classical hoplite phalanx as in later formations, but it is necessary to exercise caution as none of the surviving battle accounts mentions them. Thus, at the battle of Mantinea in 418 BC, when King Agis II of Sparta (r. 427–400 BC) turned his phalanx to the left to fight the victorious Argives (Thucydides 5.73.2), he probably ordered a 'shieldward half-turn' (90 degrees to the left), but no source gives that detail. Similarly, later orders for marching have survived; at the battle of Amphipolis (Thucydides 5.10.3–4), the Athenians were probably ordered to 'march in line to the left' (*euonumos paragoge*) or 'march in column to the left' (*euonumos epagoge*), but such details are not given in the sources.

Xenophon's *Spartan Constitution* (10.8) provides some detail. He considered that the Spartans carried out with ease the manoeuvres that instructors thought difficult, namely the forming of a line of battle from column for which the instruction might be to 'deploy into line to the left'. He claims that the Spartans could do this efficiently if an enemy appeared, yet at Mantinea (Thucydides 5.66.2) they would be thrown into consternation. Xenophon (*Spartan Constitution* 11.8–10) also gives details of phalanxes wheeling by companies and it is easy to see how such manoeuvres, which are referred to in general terms in a historical narrative, could be accomplished by issuing the orders contained within a technical manual. He notes that orders to wheel from column into line were given verbally by the *enomotarchoi*, which tallies with the chain of command provided by Thucydides (5.66.2–4) and also suggests that orders could be carried out by small units.

RECRUITMENT, TRAINING AND MOTIVATION

In both Athens and Sparta it was expected that every young man would train as a hoplite as part of his civic duty. In Athens this was restricted by wealth class, so the lower classes of citizens would train as rowers or archers instead. Some of the wealthy became cavalry although they were expected to undertake hoplite training first. Training began at the age of 18, lasted for one year and was followed by two years of patrol duty. In Sparta, every male citizen was prepared for military training from the age of seven.

Athens

For Athenian hoplite organization the modern scholar is relatively well informed, although there are issues, and one of the major sources is Aristotle's *Athenian Constitution*. Written in the 320s BC (possibly not by Aristotle), it traces the history of Athens' political reforms and assesses the state of the constitution at that time. In many cases, however, the institutions described reflect much earlier practice, so working out when such institutions were in place and exactly what they looked like can be tricky. Moreover, little information for any earlier organization exists.

Aristotle begins his summary of the contemporary form of the constitution (chapter 42 onwards) by discussing the selection of young citizens (*epheboi*) as hoplites. This reveals immediately the importance of the military institution for the Athens of the 320s BC, even after it had lost its political autonomy under the Macedonian kings. Athens' military traditions continued to exist and remained important – and what is more, there is good evidence to suggest that they existed in a form close to those described by Aristotle prior to the outbreak of the Peloponnesian War.

The sons of citizen parentage on both sides were enrolled in the rolls of the *demoi* at the age of 18 (Aristotle, *Athenian Constitution* 42.1). Eligibility for citizenship was zealously guarded in Athens and an individual had to be able to prove that both parents were citizens. Any child who was not the offspring of a citizen on both sides would be considered a *metoikos* (essentially a 'resident foreigner') and did not have the same rights as a citizen. Despite this rigour, however, Athens did not have the same issues with manpower that Sparta had, and Athens always had a large population of *metoikoi* and

Men of eligible military age were recorded by their *demos* at Athens. The 139 *demoi* of Attica were divided into ten tribes (*phulai*). Each army was drawn from particular year groups and these were divided into the ten tribal *taxeis*. These bronze identity tokens (*pinakia*), now in the collection of the Museum of the Ancient Agora, Athens, recorded the name, father's name and *demos* of Athenian citizens. (Marsyas/ Wikimedia/CC BY-SA 2.5)

xenoi ('strangers') to call upon. (Under the reforms of the Athenian statesman Cleisthenes in the late 6th century BC, Attica had 139 *demoi* and each would have lists of its men who were eligible to serve.) In addition to establishing citizen status, it is clear from the provisions described that young Athenian men attempted to enrol as an *ephebos* before they turned 18, and on several occasions (Thucydides 1.105.3–4), Athens called out the youngest and oldest men to fight (possibly those not yet serving and those over the age of enlistment). *Demoi* varied widely in size, so each would provide differing numbers for each call-up. Archanae was one of the largest, Krioa one of the smallest; in an army of 7,000, the former might provide 300 men, the latter only 14.

Once enlisted in the *epheboi*, candidates were organized by tribe (*phule*). Under Cleisthenes' reforms there were ten tribes (*phulai*) in Attica, each named after a hero of Athens: Erechtheis, Aigeis, Pandionis, Leontis, Acamantis, Oineis, Cecropis, Hippothontis, Aiantis and Antiochis. Each tribe was organized by thirds (*trittyes*), one each from the three areas of Attica – the city (*atys*), the coast (*paralia*) and the interior (*mesogeia*). This organization lasted until the late 4th century. *Demoi* and areas would therefore be mixed together under the tribal system while retaining some sense of local identity. The *epheboi* then underwent training for a year in athletics, hoplite drill and the use of javelins, bows and slings (Aristotle, *Athenian Constitution* 42.3). This training probably also involved dancing, which was recognized as being militarily useful (Plato, *Laws* 815A; Strabo 10.4.16; Xenophon, *Symposium* 2.12–14; Polybius 4.20.12). Fight trainers (*hoplomachoi*) may also have been a part of the training; their efficacy was discussed (see Plato's *Laches* and his *Laws*, 7.813D–E & 8.833E–834A, where he includes them in hoplite training). The *epheboi* messed together (*syssitia*) and after a year of training, held a drill display at the Theatre of Dionysus in Athens. To mark their graduation they each received a shield and spear from the state. For two years thereafter, aged 19–21, they went on patrol or garrison duty (*phroyros*), and were also called *peripoloi*, 'those who travel around' (Aristotle, *Athenian Constitution* 42.4–5). After their two years were up, they became members of the citizen body; wealthier citizens could presumably provide their own equipment. The names of the *epheboi* were written down on lists in the *agora* (a public open space used for markets and assemblies) under the name of the eponymous *archon* (ruler) for each year.

Athenians were eligible to serve in the military for 42 years, that is from the age of 18 to 59 (Aristotle, *Athenian Constitution* 53.4). Men over the age of 40 were eligible to be selected as trainers of the *epheboi*, three such men being elected for each of the ten tribes of Athens. From these men a disciplinary officer for each tribe would be elected and a *kosmetes*, a supervisor over all the *epheboi*, would be elected from all eligible citizens.

When the *epheboi* were enrolled, they took the ephebic oath at the Temple of Aglauros. This is recorded in several places, one such being an inscription from the *demos* of Acharnae (Rhodes & Osborne 2003: 88); this corresponds (albeit with some differences) to the version recorded by the orator Lycurgus (*Against Leocrates* 76–78 & 80–82). All these references are from the 4th century BC. In the oath, the *ephebos* swore not to bring dishonour to his arms, not to abandon his comrade in the line and to obey

The Athenian hoplite with the best-documented military career is the philosopher Socrates. This marble portrait bust is in the National Archaeological Museum, Athens. He served as a hoplite at Potidaea (433/32 BC), Delium (424 BC) and Amphipolis (422 BC). (Ann Ronan Pictures/Print Collector/Getty Images)

This funeral stele from Brauron in Attica dates from between 410 and 404 BC. Found in the eastern Attic town of Porto Rafti, it is now in the Archaeological Museum of Brauron. It shows a naked youth, Kleoboulos, with *strigil* (grooming instrument) and oil *aryballos* (flask) – wrestling accessories that may be connected with *ephebos* training. He is accompanied by an unarmoured hoplite, Menon, who wears an 'old-fashioned' Attic helmet; he also has an *aspis* and carries his *dory* by its butt-spike. (Ophelia2/Wikimedia/Public Domain)

This hoplite commander of a *lochos* leads his Athenian unit (from the Attic tribe of Leontis) against the first outpost of the Spartans on the southern end of the island of Sphacteria in the early dawn. He advances full of confidence, due not only to the element of surprise but also to the fact that his forces outnumber the Spartan hoplites 2 to 1 and the Athenians have thousands of lightly armed *psiloi* and archers – support the Spartans do not have.

Weapons, dress and equipment

This hoplite advances with his 2.4m-long *dory* (spear; **1**) made of cornel wood and tipped with an iron leaf-shaped blade (**2**). At the opposite end of the spear is a *sauroter* (literally 'lizard sticker'; **3**), made of bronze. The *sauroter* was both a counter-balance and a weapon in its own right; several surviving pieces of equipment and skulls show wounds which were made by *sauroter* blows as opposed to spear-tips. On his left hip, he wears a *xiphos* (sword; **4**) in a scabbard held in place by a baldric over his right shoulder.

His headgear is a Corinthian-style *kranos* (helmet; **5**), which fully enclosed the face except for eye slits and a narrow gap between the cheek pieces. The helmet is topped with a horsehair crest (**6**). He wears a plain suit of *linothorax* (linen armour; **7**) under which

is a *chiton* (tunic; **8**). Athenian hoplites were only provided with a shield and spear by the state and other armours would be funded by the individual. Surviving art shows that hoplites could go into battle wearing only their cloak or tunic, plain linen armour, all the way up to highly decorated linen armour and even old-fashioned 'muscled' cuirasses made of bronze. Wrapped around his left arm is his *chlamys* (cloak; **9**); this was presented to *epheboi* upon the completion of their training and is depicted in art being used in combat in various ways.

On his left arm the hoplite carries an *aspis* (shield; **10**), the main defensive tool of the hoplite. The *porpax* (arm-grip; **11**) is visible, as is the *antilabe* (hand-grip; **12**) inside the rim of the shield. His shield has a simple blazon of a capital alpha, a symbol of Athens.

This red-figure *kylix*, found in the Athenian *agora* (now in the Stoa of Attalos Museum of the Ancient Agora), shows an *ephebos* offering a libation sacrifice at an altar. His *aspis*, *dory*, helmet and cloak are obvious; he also wears a *chiton*. The *kylix* dates from *c.*480 BC (the greaves give away an early date) but suggests that *ephebos* training was already similar to that recorded in a later period. (De Agostini/Getty Images)

whoever was in authority. In Plato's *Apology* (28D–E), an elderly Socrates echoes these sentiments exactly, so much so that it suggests that he had once been an *ephebos* in the form described. Socrates argued that wherever a man stationed himself or was stationed by his commander, there he must remain and run the risks, considering neither death nor any other thing greater than disgrace. Socrates would have become eligible to be an *ephebos* *c.*451 BC. Eupolis' writings (fragment 247) suggest that he was stationed on garrison duty *c.*428 BC. Aristophanes' *Clouds* also contains the complaint (988–90) that the young men of the day – either in 423 BC or between 419 and 416 BC, when the play was produced – had neglected practising their drill and could not hold their shields properly. These references, exactly contemporary with or immediately preceding the Peloponnesian War, strongly suggest that the *epheboi* existed in the form described in the sources.

Sparta

Remarkably, the parameters for citizenship in Sparta were looser than in Athens (Plutarch, *Lycurgus* 15). The male child of a married Spartan female citizen was raised as a citizen. This is perhaps surprising, considering the importance given to full-citizen or *homoios* ('equal') status, but also, given the issue of manpower, somewhat understandable. Male children would be raised by the state to become members of the *agoge* system; Plutarch talks of children being the property of the state (*Lycurgus* 15.8).

The Spartans believed that the *agoge* system had been instituted by the legendary lawgiver Lycurgus. He remains a figure shrouded in mystery whose life dates – if he existed at all – are still disputed. The Spartan *agoge* education system was inherited from Crete (Plutarch, *Lycurgus* 4.12) and is usually described as a system of military training. In Sparta, however, it was seen more as a system which concentrated on those activities devoted to civic freedom (Xenophon, *Spartan Constitution* 7.2). Xenophon, an admirer of Sparta, praises the discipline, obedience and virtue emphasized by the Spartan *agoge* system and contrasts it with those of all other Greek cities. Plutarch characterizes the system (*Lycurgus* 16.6) as being designed to create men who obey commands, endure hardships and conquer in battle.

From the age of seven, boys (*paides*) were strictly brought up in barracks by a respected Spartan (the *paidonomos*); at the age of 17, when they became *paidiskoi*, they started to undertake military training, although their entire upbringing had led to that point. They trained until the age of 20, when they became *hebontes* (young men aged between 20 and 29) and would be voted into one of several public messes – variously called *phiditia* (Plutarch, *Lycurgus* 12.1), *syskenia* (Xenophon, *Spartan Constitution* 5.2) or *syssitia*. The messes were of mixed age groups so young men could learn virtue from the elder men. As *hebontes* they became eligible for military service. Some *hebontes* would be selected as *eirenes*, who supervised the training of *paidiskoi*. There were many similarities between the Athenian and Spartan systems, although ancient sources tend to emphasize their differences. At Sparta, too, the cloak was important – younger males were only permitted one cloak per year (Plutarch, *Lycurgus* 16.6) and a red cloak (the *phoinikis*) was part of the hoplite's 'graduation' gear (Xenophon, *Spartan Constitution* 11.3). The *phoinikis* was considered most suitable for war, along with a shield. According to Plutarch (*Spartan Customs* 24), Spartans wore red because it was considered manly, concealed wounds and terrorized inexperienced enemies.

Now in the National Archaeological Museum, Athens (Inv. 15917), this bronze Gorgon's head may have been attached to a shield as a blazon. It could be from a Spartan shield or one dedicated by a Spartan, as it was found at the temple of Athena Chalkioikos at Sparta. (Dorieo/Wikimedia/CC BY-SA 4.0)

Ancient Sparta famously had no walls – its 'walls' were its men. It was also surrounded by impressive mountain ranges, however, which kept it safe from invasion until the 4th century BC. As such, very little remains of Sparta, unlike its more flamboyant opponent, Athens. (George E. Koronaios/Wikimedia/CC BY-SA 4.0)

Spartan *enomotarchos*

This hoplite leader commands his *enomotia* of 30 men at the southern end of Sphacteria. He has taken the last watch of the night while the rest of his men catch some sleep. They have been trapped on Sphacteria for 72 days, 50 of those on only whatever food could be smuggled onto the island. He is surprised to see Athenian hoplites running at him in the early morning light but, having raised the alarm, he stands poised to take on the enemy as his training has taught him.

Weapons, dress and equipment

This hoplite wields his 2.4m-long *dory* (**1**) in an overhand posture. It has an ash shaft 5cm in diameter and is tipped by an iron blade and has a bronze *sauroter*. On his left hip he wears a *xiphos* (**2**), its blade only 35cm long. This was the standard sword of hoplites across Greece, although designs differed by region. There is much literary and archaeological evidence for shorter Spartan swords, with blades only 35cm in length, but is unclear whether this was the *encheiridion* (a shorter sword design) or simply that Spartan *xiphoi* were produced in a shorter form than those of other Greek states.

He wears a Chalkidian-style *kranos* (**3**) topped with a horsehair crest. The Chalkidian helmet has hinged cheek pieces; some pottery shows them 'open'. He is barefoot (**4**) as per the training of Spartan youths to inure them to hardship. He wears *linothorax* armour (**5**) with *pteruges* ('feathers'). He also wears his distinctive red *phoinikis* (cloak; **6**) around his arms, the cloak having been presented upon completion of his *agoge* training.

On his left arm he hefts his *aspis* (**7**) held by a *porpax* and an *antilabe*. Although it is known that some Spartan shields had a capital lambda (for 'Lacedaemonia', the Spartan heartland) emblazoned on them, this shield has a much more traditional blazon, matching those found on votive offerings in the Peloponnese; this one's swirling design matches those dedicated to the goddess Artemis Orthia at Sparta. Spartan hoplites provided their own arms and equipment, so these could vary as much as in other hoplite armies.

In both Sparta and Athens men were not considered to be full citizens until the age of 30, when they could vote and hold office. As in Athens, Spartan men were eligible for military service – and continued to train – until the age of 60. At Sparta men over 60 could also serve (see Xenophon, *Hellenica* 5.4.13, where such men are exempted). Pericles (Thucydides 2.39.1) claimed that Athens' system and training for warfare was superior to that of Sparta; Xenophon's claim (*Spartan Constitution* 11.1) is the exact opposite, that Sparta's system was best. Pericles reasoned that Athens was open to anyone and that the state educated its young to be disciplined and pursue manly courage. Interestingly, these are precisely the attributes the Spartan system was meant to imbue.

ORGANIZATION AND COMMAND

Athens

A phalanx of soldiers from the Nereid Monument, built *c.*390 BC and held at the British Museum, London (BM 874). There are eight hoplites here – one of the depths mentioned for both Spartan and Athenian phalanxes. The smallest division of the Spartan phalanx was the *enomotia* of 26–40 men; at Athens the smallest division was the *lochos*, which could have been 30 men. Neither of these numbers divides well into the shield depths when these are provided by the surviving sources. (Universal History Archive/Universal Images Group via Getty Images)

Historians are less well informed about the organization of the Athenian army than that of Sparta. It is known that there was a list of names of all those eligible for military service and that they would be selected (under their *archon* and hero-name for the year of their *ephebos* graduation) to accompany particular campaigns up to the number required (Aristotle, *Athenian Constitution* 53.7). Eligibility was usually defined as a range of years. Individuals could opt out of service; for instance, the Athenian Peisander was criticized for avoiding service, perhaps at the battle of Amphipolis (Xenophon, *Symposium* 2.12–14). When 120 of the Athenian general Demosthenes' hoplites became casualties in the Aetolia region in 426 BC, Thucydides lamented (3.98.4) that the men Athens lost were all the same age and the best men of the city, implying that the age range for this expedition was narrow and perhaps predominantly composed of younger men.

Each year, ten 'warlords' (*polemarchoi*) were elected by lot from each of the ten tribes (Aristotle, *Athenian Constitution* 55.1). The *polemarchoi* had

originally been military commanders, although they no longer held that function but instead oversaw elections and administrative affairs. All military officers were then elected by a show of hands (Aristotle, *Athenian Constitution* 43.1). The ten generals (*strategoi*) were elected from the whole body of citizens, rather than one from each tribe, which had formerly been the case (Aristotle, *Athenian Constitution* 61.1). The *strategoi* were assigned different duties: one to the hoplites, one to Attica, two to the Piraeus and one to the richest class of citizens, with the other five being assigned to campaigns as and when the need arose. The ten *taxiarchoi* (commanders of the *taxeis*) were then elected, one from each tribe, followed by the election of *lochagoi* (commanders of the *lochoi*) by the members of each tribe (Aristotle, *Athenian Constitution* 61.3). This suggests a system of ten *taxeis*, one per tribe, and then a number of *lochoi*. It is not clear how many *lochoi* there were, but they could act independently: Xenophon (*Hellenica* 1.2.3) has two operating separately in 409 BC. Given that Athenian armies were called up by year groups, the number of *lochoi* could presumably change according to each particular campaign, although in all such campaigns the troops would be organized by tribe and every Athenian army would have ten *taxeis*. The numbers in *lochoi* may have varied widely and given the large number of Athenian hoplites available it is not unrealistic to calculate that the full levy may have involved multiple *lochoi* per tribe – perhaps as many as ten when every man was called out, which happened multiple times during the Peloponnesian War. Interpretations of the strength of Athenian *lochoi* vary widely, but there is good reason to believe that the *lochos* may have numbered 30 men (see Aristophanes, *Lysistrata* 453–54). For many of the expeditions of the Peloponnesian War the sources give a specific number of thousands of hoplites (one, two or three for instance) under the command of one or more *strategoi*. In each army there would have been men from every tribe, arranged tribally in ten *taxeis* with varying strengths of *lochoi*. Corinth, Argos and Megara also used *lochoi*, as did mercenary troops, although each city-state was organized differently (see Xenophon, *Anabasis* 2.2.25, 3.4.21 & 4.7.8).

Aristotle explains that Athenian military commands could be held repeatedly, but not other offices (*Athenian Constitution* 62.3). Other sources criticize the kinds of unqualified men being selected for military commands (Aristophanes, *Wasps, Knights, Acharnians*; Eupolis, fragments 104, 293 & 384).

Sparta

The Spartan army at the time of Thucydides was organized into five *lochoi*, as it had been since the time of the Persian Wars. By the Peloponnesian War, however, the *oliganthropia* (Aristotle, *Politics* 1270A33–34) – the decline in numbers of Spartan manpower – was already apparent. Aristotle, in his lost *Constitution of the Lacedaemonians* (fragment 541), also described the 'five ancestral' *lochoi*, perhaps based on the five original villages (*obai*) which made up Sparta. The names of these five *lochoi* are given in a commentary on Aristophanes' play *Lysistrata*: *Edolos, Sinis, Arimas, Ploas* and *Messoages*. None of these names resembles those of the five villages (Limnai, Konoora, Pitana, Mesoa and Amyklai), however, and it is possible they were nicknames. Only Messoages gets close to the *oba* Mesoa.

Different sources for Spartan armies give four, six, seven or more *lochoi*. By the time of Xenophon – from 403 BC onwards (*Hellenica* 2.4.31, *Spartan Constitution* 11.4) – the sources speak not of *lochoi* but of the six *morae*, each of which may have consisted of two *lochoi*. This reform did not mean more men – just the opposite, in fact – and it possibly came about as a result of Sparta's wartime experiences. Each *mora* consisted of 600 men in two 300-strong *lochoi*. Reconciling all the different permutations into a single system is difficult, most probably because each source represented a single system at the time it was written and that system itself evolved and changed.

At the battle of Mantinea, Thucydides states (5.68.1–3) that there were seven divisions: the five *lochoi* and two additional ones, one of the latter being composed of freed helots, the *neodamodeis*, and the other of the *Brasideioi* (men of Brasidas), survivors of the Amphipolis campaign. Thucydides writes that each of these *lochoi* had four further divisions (*pentekostyes*), each commanded by a *pentekonter* or *pentekoster* (literally meaning 'commander of a fiftieth', but this cannot have been the case). There may once have been 6,400 *homoioi* at Sparta (for 'a fiftieth' to be literal); Plutarch (*Lycurgus* 8.3) records 6,000 lots of land in the original constitution. Each *pentekostys* had four *enomotiai*, each commanded by an *enomotarchos*. It is possible to calculate the strength of the Spartan army based on the other information Thucydides provides, although he begins his description with a warning of how secretive the Spartans were and that exact numbers could not be known. Thucydides relates (twice) that this was a full deployment of manpower from Sparta and that the whole army had a front rank of 448 men and an average depth of eight ranks. This suggests

The funeral stele of Alkias, now in the National Archaeological Museum of Athens (751), was found in Corinth and shows a hoplite attacking in a crouched posture, holding his spear underhand. Beneath him is the naked body of a fallen comrade. The trailing cloak is intriguing as it would presumably have been worn in the way shown here. Cloaks were important to both Athenian and Spartan hoplites, presented to them when they completed their hoplite training, and it is possible that they were used in combat to distract or entangle enemies. Several pots show cloaks wrapped around left arms when the shield is not present. (George E. Koronaios/Wikimedia/ CC BY-SA 4.0)

a phalanx of the seven *lochoi* of 3,584 men. These numbers therefore suggest that each *lochos* had 512 men, each 'fiftieth' had 128 men and each *enomotia* had 32 men. The exact number in each *enomotia* is debatable, however, and different accounts suggest different numbers. It is more likely that it was never precise. At Mantinea, one-sixth of the men (the oldest and youngest) were sent home to guard the city (Thucydides 5.64.3) and so each of these units lost some of its manpower, implying that they fought on at less than their full strength. The *Suda* (E, 1408) states that the *enomotia* had 25 men, whereas on the island of Sphacteria in 425 BC the 420 hoplites of the garrison could have

This red-figure *kylix*, now in the Staatliche Antikensammlungen, Munich (Inv. 2688/J 370), shows Achilles slaying the Amazon queen Penthesilea. Dating from 460 BC, it shows in detail the sword and scabbard, the bowl of Achilles' *aspis* and details of helmet decoration. The figure on the left seems to carry a lighter javelin rather than a *dory*. (Culture Club/ Getty Images)

been 12 units of 35 or 14 of 30 (see below for a different analysis). If these units were understrength, it amounts to the usual eight *enomotiai* with only 26 men each – very close to the *Suda*'s number.

The picture is further complicated by Xenophon, writing later, who may have been taking a dig at Thucydides by saying the Spartan system was not complicated at all. Xenophon includes an account of the organization of the Spartan army in his *Spartan Constitution* (11). There, and in his continuation of Thucydides' history, the *Hellenica* (2.4.31), Xenophon introduces the idea that the Spartan army was organized into six *morae*, each commanded by a *polemarchos*, and relates that each *mora* had four *lochagoi*, eight *pentekonteres* and 16 *enomotarachoi* (*Constitution* 11.4–10). Except for the *mora* this roughly matches Thucydides' description, although Thucydides has 32 men per *enomotiai*. Xenophon further explains that, when given the order, these *morae* would form abreast, sometimes two, sometimes three, sometimes six in number. Xenophon's *enomotiai* have 36 men each (*Hellenica* 6.4.12, 17). Many scholars have rejected Thucydides' information in favour of Xenophon's but there is no reason to do so; Thucydides provides a coherent picture in 418 BC.

All of this implies that there was some kind of reform of the Spartan system after Mantinea, although some scholars have sought to reconcile Xenophon's system with Thucydides' description of the battle. Also, there was no crisis like Sphacteria after Mantinea until the battle of Leuctra in 371 BC, but Xenophon's system seems to have been in place by 403 BC. Thucydides never uses the term 'mora' and in Book 7 of the *Hellenica*, Xenophon reverts to *lochos* although he refers to 12 *lochoi* (*Hellenica* 7.4.20 & 7.5.10), implying that each *mora* had two *lochoi* but the *mora* had only 600 men. In this case, Xenophon's four *lochagoi* must be an error and there were in fact two. Book 7, however, deals with events in the 360s BC. It is possible that military reform happened after the disaster of Sphacteria and the threat to Spartan manpower;

perhaps it was in place by Mantinea, where there were *polemarchoi* and more than five *lochoi*. It is also possible that the presence of Brasidas' veterans or the need to recruit *neodamodeis* became the impetus for the presence of a sixth division (*mora*), its inclusion meaning that the traditional five *lochoi* were supplanted by six *morae*. Such changes may have taken time to implement, and it is possible that Thucydides was unaware of (or incorrectly informed about) them. Later divisions may also have been a way of mitigating threats to Spartan manpower. Another fragment of Aristotle's *Constitution of the Lacedaemonians* (fragment 540, *Suda* 1259) confirms that there were six *morae* and that all of Sparta's men were divided among them.

As far as it is possible to tell, Spartan commanders (except the king himself) were selected rather than elected. At Sphacteria (Thucydides 4.38.1–2), when the Spartan commander, Epitadas, was slain during the fighting, Hippagretas was selected to replace him. He too fell (but was not killed) and so a third man, Styphon, originally chosen to command if anything happened to the first two choices, took command. When Brasidas died at Amphipolis, Clearidas was his designated second, which implies that such succession of command was usual practice.

In Sparta, too, men were levied for each expedition (Xenophon, *Spartan Constitution* 11.2). The senior magistrates (*ephoroi*) would issue a proclamation with the age limit for the levy which would include infantry, cavalry, and the men needed to accompany the campaign, the artisans (*cheirotechnais*).

In the Spartan system, and perhaps for Athens too, there were file leaders and file closers. These were usually the best men (Xenophon, *Memorabilia* 3.1.8) and the sources relate that they were all 'officers' (*archontes*, meaning leader but not a specific rank: Xenophon, *Spartan Constitution* 11.5). These file leaders and closers are odd, however, since the depth of a formation does not seem to have been standard, differing by battle and even varying between different units involved in the same battle. In each case there would have been file leaders and file closers, but not as many in deeper formations.

On campaign, the armies of both Athens and Sparta messed in much smaller groups. According to Xenophon (*Spartan Constitution* 13.1), on campaign the Spartan king shared a tent with the six *polemarchoi* (the commanders of the *morae*) and three others, implying a tent of ten men. The rest of the Spartan army may have followed a similar pattern, although according to Plutarch (*Lycurgus* 12.2), mess-mates at Sparta numbered 15 or fewer. Plato explains that Athenians messed together on campaign (*Symposium* 219E–220D), but it is not clear how many men shared a tent.

This bronze *pilos* helmet dating from the period of the Peloponnesian War and now in the Metropolitan Museum of Art, New York (08.258.14), shows the simple design of such headgear. Hammered bronze examples of these helmets could be produced much more cheaply and quickly than other designs. The holes may have been used to tie a chinstrap or display the helmet as an offering. (Metropolitan Museum of Art/Wikimedia/CC0)

MANPOWER

Athens

Just prior to his famous funeral speech (Thucydides 2.34–46) honouring those men of Athens who had died in the first year of the Peloponnesian War (431/430 BC), Pericles, elected as one of the ten *strategoi* in 430 BC, outlined the resources and number of men available for Athens' defence (2.13.6–8). Pericles refers to Athens' four corps: hoplites, cavalry, navy and archers. Athenian archers were paid all year round; they served aboard triremes, but could also fight on land as at Sphacteria. Athens had 13,000 hoplites plus an additional 16,000 on garrison duty and manning the city walls; these 16,000 were the oldest and youngest citizens and *metoikoi*. The city walls were guarded along 43 *stadia* of their length (one *stadion* being equivalent to 184.9m) as were the walls to the Piraeus (the port in which the Athenian navy was based) along another 40 *stadia*, and the walls around the Piraeus another 60 *stadia*. Guards therefore manned more than 27km of wall (at roughly one man per 1.65m). The cavalry corps numbered 1,200 men and the archer corps 1,600. Athens had 300 seaworthy triremes each of which carried 14 hoplites and four archers, thus accounting for 4,200 of the hoplites and 1,200 of the archer corps. Each trireme had a crew of 200 rowers, drawn from three pools of manpower. While the poorest citizen class, the *thetes*, contributed perhaps 80 rowers per trireme, 60 more rowers were *metoikoi* and the remaining 60 were *xenoi*. These numbers suggest a total of 24,000 citizen rowers and 18,000 each of *metoikoi* and *xenoi*. Such men would have fought as *psiloi* on campaigns in which the troops were transported by ships, such as at Sphacteria and Amphipolis.

Athens' seemingly vast manpower resources can be contrasted with those of Sparta: Athens had 29,000 hoplites available whereas Sparta had only 4,000. The fact that 13,000 hoplites were apparently outnumbered by the combined total of the oldest and youngest (and *metoikoi*) has long worried scholars. If it is assumed that 50 per cent of the 16,000 hoplites who guarded the walls were *metoikoi* – which may be too high a figure, although Thucydides (2.31.2) reveals that there were at least 3,000 *metoikoi* – this still gives a figure of 21,000 eligible Athenian citizen hoplites. Sparta would have had to rely upon hoplites from among its allies and *perioeci* (and later by enfranchising freed helots) to swell its numbers. This was something Pericles recognized (Thucydides 2.39.2). Athens too had to rely on mercenaries, especially cavalry and archers (Thucydides 2.22.3 & 6.25.2).

The total population of Athens (and therefore Attica) in 431 BC has been estimated at 50,000 male citizens, 25,000 male *metoikoi* and 100,000 slaves, but this last figure may be far too low. Herodotus (5.97.3) recorded that Athens before the battle of Marathon in 490 BC had 30,000 citizens, but this figure has been challenged. After the Persian Wars, the population of Athens grew; estimates put the total citizen population at 140,000–150,000 including women, children and the elderly. When the Athenian fleet in 431 BC (24,000 citizen rowers), hoplites (perhaps 21,000) and then 1,200 cavalry and 1,600 archers are considered – a total figure of 47,800 – 50,000 male citizens does not seem unrealistic. To get this number each *demos* needed to provide, on average, 151 men.

In 309/308 BC, after a period of decline, Demetrius of Phalerum carried out a census in Attica (Athenaeus 6.272C), which put the population at 21,000 male citizens, 10,000 male *metoikoi* and 400,000 slaves. Xenophon recorded that, during the Peloponnesian War, Nicias owned 1,000 slaves, Hipponicus 600 and Philemonides 300 (*Ways and Means* 4.14–15), and so a figure of closer to 1,000,000 slaves in 431 BC might be more accurate. This latter figure might sound inconceivable, but it is the same ratio of 20 slaves per male citizen as in 309/308 BC. Athens was the largest city in Greece by far and even the much smaller Aegina had 470,000 slaves. These slaves were working on farms and in mines and not all would have been brought into the city during the Spartan invasions.

In 413 BC, when the Spartans occupied the town of Decelea in Attica, more than 20,000 slaves deserted (Thucydides 7.27.5). This was disastrous but cannot have represented one-fifth of the total slaves in Attica. The population of male *metoikoi* (18,000 rowers and approximately 8,000 hoplites) might mean 25,000 is also too low a figure since they, no doubt, undertook other tasks although they could not own property and held few rights (some estimates place their total number at 70,000). The plague killed one-quarter of this population, which suggests a death toll of between 55,000 and 75,000 citizens and *metoikoi* from a total of around 220,000–300,000. Thucydides explains that the plague killed no fewer than 4,400 hoplites and 300 cavalry in 426 BC (3.87.3). Despite these horrendous losses, Athens' population seems to have bounced back remarkably quickly. At the battle of Delium in 424 BC, Athens summoned every available hoplite, though this only amounted to a total of 7,000 (Thucydides 4.93.3–94.1). At Amphipolis and Mantinea Athens' total available citizen hoplite numbers cannot have numbered many more that 6,000, although it should be noted that the same command structure remained as when Athens had had four times that many. Just three years later, Athens could once again raise an army of 50,000 for the Sicilian expedition of 415–413 BC including ships' crews and 5,000 citizen hoplites (Thucydides 6.43, 7.16.2 & 7.42.1). When the final disaster in Sicily befell them in 431 BC, Athens could lose these men (7.75.5–7.85.3) and still fight on until the end of the war in 404 BC.

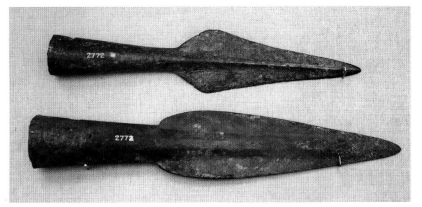

These bronze spearheads from Olympia in the Peloponnese correspond to those depicted on sculpture and pottery. The design of spearheads did not go through any fundamental change in the 5th century BC. (Universal History Archive/Universal Images Group via Getty Images)

Sparta

The kind of information for Athens is not available for Sparta, although using the calculation of the total militarily eligible male population at Mantinea (4,000), it is possible to estimate a total male citizen Spartan population of perhaps 12,000. This was augmented by the *perioeci* – the populations of the cities of Laconia – and the helots of Laconia and Messenia, as well as allied cities. The total population of Sparta – which had a large non-citizen population, because citizens were forbidden to operate businesses, thus requiring non-citizens to provide every form of goods and services – has been estimated at 40,000–50,000 and the total of the region of Lacedaemonia at 135,000–155,000. Estimates of helot numbers are difficult to ascertain; according to Herodotus (9.10.1), at Plataea there were 5,000 hoplites and 35,000 helots, so seven helots for every hoplite, and many more must have stayed in Sparta. The total helot population for Sparta is estimated to have been about 200,000. The total number of *perioeci* is unknown and it is necessary to interrogate individual accounts; at Sphacteria, for example, Spartan citizen hoplites may have made up 40 per cent of the total Spartan force, with *perioeci* and Peloponnesian hoplites providing the balance of 60 per cent. It is possible they outnumbered the *homoioi* by 3 to 1 or even 5 to 1. Nevertheless, Attica alone was almost as populous as the entire alliance Sparta could bring against it.

Data relating to other cities can also be informative, and serve to show how large Athens was in comparison to its neighbours. Lysias (34.7) records that in 400 BC, the city of Mantinea had fewer than 3,000 adult male citizens out of a total population of about 21,000; and that the Argives numbered no more than Athens (but did not have the same foreign population or land mass), so perhaps 6,000 adult males at that time (after all of Athens' losses) and thus a total population of 18,000 plus slaves. It is possible that Spartan men in their twenties outnumbered men in their fifties by 2 to 1.

Like the spearhead, the design of the *dory*'s butt-spike remained largely unchanged for centuries. Now in the Metropolitan Museum of Art, New York (74.51.5319), this example from Cyprus is remarkably similar to examples found in Olympia and dating to the 5th century BC, which are inscribed and were left as dedications. (Metropolitan Museum of Art/ Wikimedia/CC0)

Sphacteria

425 BC

BACKGROUND TO BATTLE

Despite the clear numerical advantage Athens had over Sparta in manpower, Pericles encouraged a policy of defensive action (Thucydides 2.13.2 & 2.39.2). At the conclusion of the first year of the Peloponnesian War, Pericles was selected to give a funeral speech honouring Athens' war dead (Thucydides 2.35.1–46.2). Pericles compared Athens with Sparta (although Sparta is unnamed) and on all points found Athens superior, especially in that Athenian decisions rested with the many, rather than the few, meaning they were made by the entire citizen body and not by a few magistrates as in Sparta. As Pericles had foreseen, Athens' population bridled at not responding to Spartan aggression against Attica. In 430 BC the people turned on Pericles, blaming him for the war (Thucydides 2.59) and fining him (Thucydides 2.65.3). Thucydides does not give the value of the fine, but both Plutarch (*Pericles* 35) and Diodorus (12.45) give differing values. Despite fining him, however, the Athenians then returned Pericles to office as *strategos* for another year.

The Spartan occupations of Attica, of which there were five in the first phase of the war – the ten-year-long Archidamian War (431–421 BC), named after the Spartan king Archidamus II (r. *c.*476–427) – were brief in duration: the longest of them (in 430 BC) lasted just 40 days, the shortest (in 425 BC) 15 days. In 429 BC there was no invasion at all (Thucydides 2.71), Archidamus II instead marching against the city of Plataea in Boeotia and putting it under siege; it fell in 427 BC. This was an attempt to lure Athenian forces out to fight for their ally, but Athens resisted. That year also showed the wisdom of Pericles' policy as an Athenian army, having taken Potidaea after a three-year siege, was defeated at Spartolus in Thrace by the Chalcidians (Thucydides

2.79). The Athenian navy, commanded by Phormio, did enjoy success against a Corinthian fleet more than twice its size (Thucydides 2.83–84). The Athenian ships literally rowed circles around the Corinthians whose ships became fouled with one another, and when Phormio gave the order to charge, the Athenian navy easily sank several Corinthian ships and captured a further 12 (Thucydides 2.84.4). This action amply showed the superiority of Athenian naval power and ship handling.

Sparta also suffered a setback the same year trying to subdue the city of Stratus in Acarnania (Thucydides 2.81): it was to Stratus that the Corinthian fleet had been travelling. This action almost escalated into a wider engagement. Unable to comprehend how the larger Corinthian fleet had been defeated by so few Athenian ships, Sparta sent more naval reinforcements, commanded by Brasidas son of Tellis, Timocrates and Lycophron. The Peloponnesian fleet now numbered 77 ships (with 1,000 hoplites assisting on the shore), the Athenians still mustering only 20 vessels, as sufficient personnel to man the 12 captured Corinthian ships were not available. Another 20 Athenian ships had been delayed by a punitive action on Crete (Thucydides 2.86).

After a week of posturing, a remarkable see-saw battle took place near the port of Naupactus in Aetolia (Thucydides 2.90.1–92.2); the Athenians initially lost nine ships but were able to reverse their fortunes so that they recovered the lost ships and captured six of the Peloponnesian vessels. Nevertheless, before the year was out but with winter already begun, Brasidas launched a daring raid against the Piraeus, marching his rowers overland from Corinth to Megara and there embarking on fresh ships (Thucydides 2.93.2). The breathtaking (and almost un-Spartan) daring exhibited by Brasidas was something the Athenians would see again. Thucydides relates that the Piraeus was unguarded – why would it be when Athens was so superior at sea – but no ships were left in the harbour. Athens was alerted by fire signal (2.94.1) and the ensuing panic was the worst seen in the Peloponnesian War until 411 BC, when an oligarchic coup briefly overthrew the democracy. The Spartan raid did not take the Piraeus due to contrary winds and every man in Athens manning every available ship to make a show of force. Brasidas was, however, able to ravage the island of Salamis. This daring raid prompted Athens take measures to protect the Piraeus in future (2.94.4).

Pericles' death in September 429 BC – from the plague which inevitably followed such a large population withdrawing into the cramped conditions behind Athens' walls – was probably the greatest disaster to befall Athens during the war. He would have already been dead by the time of Brasidas' raid on the Piraeus and his death must have added to the panic evident in Athens.

The see-sawing brinkmanship of encounters like those in 429 BC continued for the first years of the Peloponnesian War and set up a pattern of small-scale encounters which threatened to escalate into a larger conflict. It was very much a tit-for-tat war and these clashes were acts of opportunism for both sides: had any one of them gone a different way, it would have charted a different course for the war. If the Spartan navy had been victorious in its raid on the Piraeus and gained more confidence as a result, Athens' position of supremacy on the sea would have been challenged. If Athens defeated a Spartan force on land, the Athenians would in turn become more confident and prepare to face the Spartan hoplites again – and in the course

Now in the Vatican (Inv. 269), this bust of Pericles, son of Xanthippus, is a Roman copy of a Greek original dating to about 430 BC. Before war broke out, Pericles had counselled that when Sparta and its allies marched against Attica – which it was suspected they would do – the population of Attica should withdraw behind the walls of Athens (Thucydides 1.143.1–5). Most important to Pericles and to Athens was control of the sea. When Sparta marched against Athens, the Athenian navy would sail against Sparta. The Athenians, Pericles advised, should relinquish their land and strive to protect the city and the sea. Athens' population should not give way to resentment against the attacks the Spartans would make upon its farms and land and risk a decisive land battle because, if Athens lost such a battle, it would lose control of its seaborne allies, and that the Athenians could not afford. This policy, and Pericles' ability to persuade the people of Athens to follow it, is truly remarkable. Perhaps Pericles' most perceptive insight was that he feared Athens' own mistakes more than the plans of the enemy (Thucydides 1.144.1). Had Pericles lived, and if Athens had continued to follow his policies, Athens would probably have prevailed in the war and Sparta would have exhausted itself in futile raids. (CM Dixon/Print Collector/Getty Images)

of the war to 426 BC and at Pylos and Sphacteria in 425 BC, that is exactly what happened.

Before that, however, in 428 BC, the familiar pattern continued despite a power vacuum in Athenian leadership. There were ample numbers of men willing to try to fill Pericles' shoes, but none was as capable as he. Despite this, they more or less continued with Pericles' policies. Archidamus II led a raid into Attica once more (again with two-thirds of his full contingent), this one early, as the grain was ripening rather than already gathered. Once again, Athenian cavalry harassed the Spartans to mitigate the effects of the raids (Thucydides 3.1.1–2). When their supplies ran out, the Spartans returned to the Peloponnese.

Something then happened that was eventually to contribute to Athens' downfall: one of its allies revolted. In 428 BC it was Lesbos, one of the most important island member states, and this prevented the Athenians from sending the usual large fleet to raid the Peloponnese. Instead they despatched a fleet to the city of Mytilene on Lesbos and a much smaller fleet around the Peloponnese, which met with no success. A truce was agreed but meanwhile, the Mytilenaeans entered into an alliance with Sparta (Thucydides 3.15.1).

Somewhat uncharacteristically, the Spartans launched another invasion of Attica, planning to attack by both land and sea, this time dragging their ships themselves across the isthmus of Corinth. To retaliate, Athens manned 100 ships with its entire citizen body and population of *metoikoi* (the two highest wealth classes were exempt). These operated as a show of force and launched raids on the Peloponnese. They also had the desired effect on Archidamus II and the Spartans, who considered that they had underestimated Athens' naval strength. One ramification of all this, however, was that Athens had to pay everyone serving it in these extraordinary circumstances, which depleted the Athenian coffers. Hoplites, rowers and skilled workers were each paid one drachma per day (Thucydides 3.17.3) and in 428 BC Athens was manning 250 triremes (at least 55,000 men). This added to the costs of the three-year siege of Potidaea, during which the troops, maintained at 3,000 throughout, were paid for the entire time they were on campaign. Such extreme ongoing costs had not been anticipated at the start of the war.

The year 427 BC saw another invasion of Attica and a Spartan fleet sent to help Mytilene, but it proved ineffective. In a sign of the dangers to come, those Athenians eligible to vote – male citizens over the age of 30 – voted to execute the entire adult male population of Mytilene before having a change of heart and sending a fast ship to overtake the one despatched with the original decision (Thucydides 3.25–50). Sparta finally captured Plataea and executed the remaining garrison (most had escaped during the winter of 428/427 BC). A civil war on the island of Corcyra acted as another opportunity for the conflict between Athens and Sparta to escalate but again, 12 Athenian ships saw off an attack by 33 Spartan ships and further reinforcements on both sides meant nothing further was attempted. The ferocity of the war also escalated – Thucydides relates that the first atrocities of the war were committed on Corcyra (Thucydides 3.84.1). Athens also offered help to the city of Leontini on Sicily against Syracuse, sending 20 ships.

One sign of the conservative and stable nature of the Sparta regime came with the death of Archidamus II in 427 BC (it is not clear precisely when).

Rather than this being a disaster for Sparta, like Pericles' death was for Athens, the succession of his son, Agis II (r. 427–*c*.400 BC), was smooth and it was he who would lead the invasion of 426 BC. That year, however, the Spartan invasion force turned back because of earthquakes and instead, Sparta established a colony at Heracleia close to Thermopylae, thus making it possible for Sparta to harass Euboea and the grain route to and from Thrace. Athens was distracted by facing Thebes' army at Tangara in Boeotia (Thucydides 3.91.3–6) but, fortunately for the Athenians, prevailed. Athens also sent 60 ships against the island of Melos.

Meanwhile, the ambitious Athenian *strategos* Demosthenes, in the Corinthian Gulf with 30 ships (Thucydides 3.91), was meant to be aiding the Acarnanians but saw an opportunity for personal glory and so turned against Aetolia. At first, he easily took several cities (Thucydides 3.94.3). The Acarnanians, however, having been rebuffed, refused to assist him. Demosthenes then took Aegitium but was attacked by missile troops who refused to engage with his heavy infantry – and he only had the 120 archers from his small fleet; they fired until their arrows were exhausted. Retreating, Demosthenes, who was by now without a guide, got lost and his army, now fleeing, was attacked and cut down by mobile Aetolian missile troops. They killed 120 of Demosthenes' 420 hoplites and most of his allies. The remainder sailed back to Athens but Demosthenes remained in Naupactus, fearful of what he might be convicted of by a vengeful Athenian *demos* (Thucydides 3.98.5).

On Sicily, the Athenian *strategos* Laches met with setbacks and instead raided Locris. The Spartans, led by Eurylochus and Macarius, marched against Naupactus with 3,000 hoplites, including 600 from Heracleia (Thucydides 3.100.2), but Demosthenes, fielding an Acarnanian force, dissuaded them from assaulting the port's walls. Later that year, near Olpae in Acarnania, Demosthenes took an allied force of 200 Messenians, 1,000 Acarnanians and Amphilochians and the men from only 20 Athenian ships (barely 60 archers) and defeated a numerically superior force of 3,000 Spartans plus their allies from Ambracia and Mantinea. Demosthenes stationed 400 of his troops (a mix of hoplites and *psiloi*) in a sunken ravine and these attacked the rear of the Spartans after they had begun to encircle the remainder of Demosthenes' troops. The Spartans were routed. Seeing the best Spartan troops and both commanders cut down, the allied forces fled. This battle showed that the Spartans could be beaten, even when they outnumbered the enemy. Luckily for Demosthenes, his reputation was restored, even enhanced, and he had gained the self-confidence to face Spartan hoplites. The following year he would put these lessons into practice.

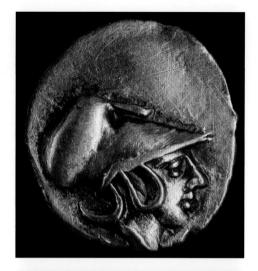

Sea power facilitated the spread of Greek culture and communities across the Mediterranean. This 4th-century BC coin from Emporion in Spain and now in the State Hermitage Museum, St Petersburg, shows Athena in a Corinthian helmet and, on the reverse, a cavalryman whose cloak is evident (other examples show Pegasus). Emporion (meaning 'trading place') was founded in 575 BC at the end of a period of massive Greek colonization. (Fine Art Images/Heritage Images/Getty Images)

MAP KEY

1 The Athenians embark their forces on the fleet's triremes in the night. Landing before dawn at the southern end of the island, on both the eastern and the western sides, they achieve complete surprise. The Spartans have their main camp in the centre of the island, near the spring, consisting of around 375 hoplites and 200 helots. There is also a small Spartan contingent, less than an *enomotia* of 30 men, in the ruined fort at the northern end of the island. Stationed at the southern end of the island is a guard post of a single *enomotia*.

2 The Athenians land and immediately charge the southern Spartan guard post and overwhelm it.

3 The Athenians draw up their line of 800 hoplites in ten tribal *taxeis*, each of 80 men; the rightmost *taxis* is Demosthenes' (as he is *strategos* along with Cleon) with his *taxis* of the tribe Aiantis (**A**); Cleon himself is on the left of the Athenian line with his *taxis* of Pandionis (**B**). To the left of the Athenian formation is a single *lochos* of Messenian hoplites, 40 strong (**C**). On both flanks of the Athenians are contingents of archers and peltasts brought by Cleon (**D**); and behind all of these are the lightly armed *psiloi* of the Athenians and the crews of the 70-plus ships armed with whatever they can find (**E**). Two companies of Messenian archers and *psiloi* (**F**) are detached to scale the heights up to the position of the fort, the Spartans' last-stand position.

4 The Athenian formation advances on the main Spartan camp; their adversaries are now aware of the Athenians' landing. The Spartans draw up their remaining forces in ten *enomotia*, five of Spartan citizens (**G**) and five of Peloponnesians (**H**). Behind these the helots (**I**) operate as lightly armed troops. The Spartan commander Epitadas, in the centre of the Spartan line, advances against the Athenian hoplites.

5 The Athenians do not engage with their hoplites but instead use their overwhelming superiority in missile troops to harass the Spartans. The Spartan hoplites advance against the Athenian missile troops, but the more lightly armed Athenians withdraw. Emboldened by their successes, the Athenian missile troops become more audacious, drawing closer and closer to the Spartan hoplite formation.

6 Finally, the Athenian hoplites close with the Spartans and surround them. The Spartans close ranks and withdraw to the site of the fort. There the newly confident Athenians make a frontal assault and the battle continues for some time.

7 The Messenian archers and *psiloi* under Comon complete their ascent of the heights at the northern end of the island and are able to attack the Spartans in the fort from behind. This new attack and renewed assaults by the remainder of the Athenian forces spells the end for the 292 remaining Spartans and Peloponnesians.

Battlefield environment

According to Thucydides (4.8.6), the island of Sphacteria or Sphagia was almost 15 *stadia* (2.8km) long. At its widest point, it was barely 500m wide. The passage between its northern end and the site of Pylos would only permit two ships to pass abreast; at its southern end, only eight or nine ships could travel abreast. The site of the battle is usually identified with the island in the modern-day Bay of Pylos (or Navarino) but the southern channel is vastly wider, perhaps challenging Thucydides' reputation for accuracy – but it is very unlikely Thucydides ever saw the place. The alternative site of Coryphasium (modern-day Palaeo-Kastro) does not pass muster,

however; the distances involved and the area available for battle simply do not work.

Sphacteria was covered in trees, uninhabited and without roads. Just prior to the Athenian assault, however, a fire swept the island, denuding it of trees (it remains relatively treeless today). At its higher, northern end, a steep rocky precipice looked down towards Pylos. At the centre of the island lay a relatively flat plateau and at the southern end, the island tapered down to the sea. Only here and on its landward side were there suitable places for a landing to take place, although being on the seaward side such a landing was still dangerous.

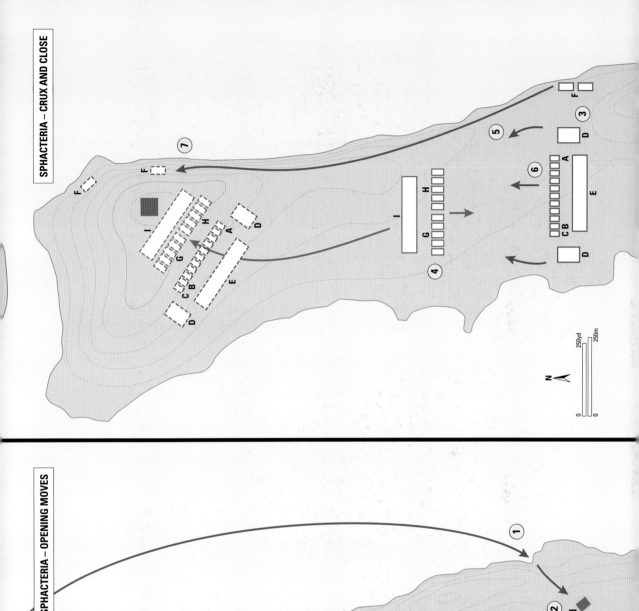

SPHACTERIA – CRUX AND CLOSE

SPHACTERIA – OPENING MOVES

Pylos

Fort

S P H A C T E R I A

Spartan camp

Spring

Guard post

INTO COMBAT

The year 425 BC began with an eruption of Mount Aetna on Sicily and the revolt of Messana against Athens' control. Once again, before the fields of grain ripened, the Spartans led by Agis II invaded Attica. Athens despatched 40 ships to Sicily with the *strategoi* Sophocles and Eurymedon, to assist Corcyra en route. Demosthenes was also assigned 40 ships to harass the coast of the Peloponnese (Thucydides 4.1–2). Rounding the south-western corner of the Peloponnesian coast, Sophocles and Eurymedon wanted to press on to Corcyra, but Demosthenes convinced them to put in at Pylos (a convenient storm helped to persuade them to do so). Demosthenes advocated fortifying the spot using the local natural resources. Pylos was only 75km from Sparta and posed enough of a threat to ensure that, in Athenian hands, it could not be ignored. It had a natural harbour protected by the island of Sphacteria; it was also close to Messenia, homeland of the helots, and an Athenian presence could encourage them to revolt against their masters. The *strategoi* and other army commanders remained unconvinced of Demosthenes' plan but, unsure of what action to take, they stayed at Pylos. It therefore fell to the soldiers themselves who, with nothing else to do, began to fortify the place, essentially building a drywall fortress in six days (Thucydides 4.4.1–5.2). Diodorus relates that the construction work took 20 days (12.61.1). This was all done while the Spartan invasion of Attica was still under way; the remainder of the Spartans thought that the Athenians would flee if they approached. Demosthenes was then left with only five ships and the majority of the Athenian fleet sailed on to Corcyra and Sicily, their original destination.

As soon as the Spartans in Attica heard of the occupation of Pylos, they hastened to return home; they had been in Attica only 15 days (Thucydides 4.6.1–2). Once they returned, the Spartans and *perioeci* made their way to relieve Pylos. The 60 Spartan ships at Corcyra were also summoned; the Spartans avoided detection by the Athenian fleet sailing north by hauling their fleet across the isthmus of Leucas (Thucydides 4.8.2). Demosthenes sent two of his triremes with a request for assistance to another Athenian fleet stationed at the island of Zacynthus. The Spartans then transported some hoplites across to the uninhabited island of Sphacteria to fortify it against occupation by more Athenians. This robbed the Athenians at Pylos of a place to beach their ships, because there was nowhere suitable on the coast of the mainland.

Thucydides relates (4.8.9) that the Spartan hoplites transferred across to Sphacteria numbered 420. They were selected by lot from all the companies (*lochoi*) and commanded by Epitadas son of Molobrus. Helots also accompanied this force, but no number is given for them; their numbers could range from one helot per Spartan hoplite up to seven per hoplite, as at Plataea, but it was probably not that high a number. Prior to the arrival of this force, Spartan detachments had occupied the island and relieved one another, but this force would be the last. Analysing the breakdown of the prisoners captured on the island makes it possible to extrapolate other information. Thucydides gives very exact numbers (4.38.5): of the 420 hoplites on the island, 292 were taken to Athens as prisoners, 120 of whom were full Spartan citizens. The other 172 hoplites were therefore not full citizens but *perioeci*.

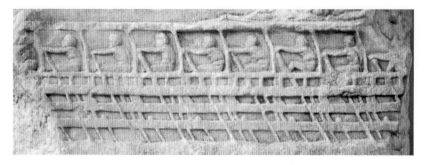

The Lenormant relief, depicting oarsmen on an Athenian warship and dating from 410–400 BC, is on display at the Museum at the Acropolis in Athens (Inv. 1339). Rowers such as these fought alongside the hoplites in battle, armed with whatever came to hand. (Ann Johansson/Corbis via Getty Images)

The helots who accompanied the force are not mentioned (it is unlikely they would be mentioned as prisoners). This breakdown reinforces the idea that the garrison was a collection of *enomotiai* selected by lot rather than a full *lochos*. If these ratios are applied to the remainder of the force of 420 hoplites it is possible to posit that full Spartan citizens had made up 40 per cent of the garrison, so 172 hoplites, and the non-citizens 60 per cent, or 248 hoplites. A minimum of 172 helots therefore probably accompanied the Spartan hoplites. The garrison was therefore six understrength Spartan *enomotiai* of 28 or 29 men each and eight almost full-strength non-Spartan *enomotiai*, which provides the same 40:60 ratio.

Before a land operation could be attempted, Demosthenes had to respond to the threat from the sea. He drew up his remaining three triremes on the shore, put a barricade around them and armed their crews with shields, most of which were made of plaited willow (Thucydides 4.9.1). A passing Messenian ship provided these men with arms and landed another 40 hoplites, although some of Demosthenes' men remained unarmed. Most of these troops he positioned on the newly built fortifications facing inland, towards the direction of a land attack from the Spartan camp. With 60 hoplites and some archers (his three triremes would only have provided 12, but he seems to have had 400 in total), Demosthenes manned the weakest point of his fortifications on the seaward side.

After a speech by Demosthenes (Thucydides 4.10) encouraging the Athenians to stand their ground, the Spartans launched an attack by land and sea using 43 triremes, but is difficult to accept Diodorus' number of 12,000 hoplites (12.61.2) for the land assault. Demosthenes had chosen his ground well and the Spartans attacked just where Demosthenes expected they would. Demosthenes' words of encouragement to his troops were also prophetic because the ground was rocky and treacherous as he had said and the Spartans could only attack the fortifications in small detachments. One of the Spartan naval captains, Brasidas, showed himself to be the bravest of all, driving his ship aground in order to attack the Athenians (Thucydides 4.11.3–12.1; Diodorus 12.62.1–5). He led the way but fainted after receiving many wounds; his shield was captured and dedicated as a trophy by the Athenians. Thucydides notes the irony that the Spartans were fighting from their ships while the Athenians were fighting on land – and Spartan land to boot (Thucydides 4.12.3 & 4.14.3–4). The Athenians stood firm and the Spartans could not dislodge them.

These attacks went on for two days, after which the Spartans sought to build siege engines, but the arrival of the 50-ship Athenian fleet from

Zacynthus forestalled that. The Spartans, seeing the arrival of a fleet slightly larger than their own, did not intend to put to sea and risk a naval battle but stayed within the harbour, camping on the shore opposite Sphacteria (Thucydides 4.13.4). The Athenian fleet therefore rowed into the harbour via both entrances and attacked the Spartan fleet, capturing five of the Spartan ships and ramming others, even as they lay hauled up on the beach. As the Athenians began to haul away the hulks, Spartan hoplites from the camp ran into the water fully armoured and attempted to drag their ships back ashore (Thucydides 4.14.1). They recovered some ships, but the Athenians had the better of the engagement and now began to patrol around the island to ensure that no relief came to the garrison and no one could escape.

When news of the trapped garrison on Sphacteria reached Sparta, the magistrates went to the Spartan camp to see the disaster for themselves. Observing the dire situation, they proposed a truce whereby they would surrender to the Athenians their entire fleet of 60 triremes and the Athenians would allow them to supply the Sphacteria garrison with provisions (Thucydides 4.16.1). They would also refrain from attacking the Athenian fortifications and the Athenians would undertake not to attack the island or the Spartan camp on the mainland. The truce would last while Spartan envoys travelled to Athens to sue for peace. When the envoys returned, the Athenians would return the Spartan ships. At this point, if the proposed ratios are correct, 172 full Spartan citizens were on Sphacteria. The threat of the loss of this few citizens was enough to force Sparta to sue for peace. It is important to note the fragility of the Spartan system. If the threat of losing this (small) number of hoplites could cause such consternation, it should have been a clear sign to Athens to increase the frequency of attacks against the Spartan garrisons, taking even more prisoners. Instead, Athens squandered the opportunity and became distracted by other projects, such as fighting Thebes. Nevertheless, Athens by contrast could afford to lose thousands of men – such as at Syracuse in 413 BC (Thucydides 7.75) – and still fight on.

The Spartan envoys visiting Athens proposed peace (Thucydides 4.19) in return for the release of their men stranded on Sphacteria. The Athenians had wanted peace when plague ravaged Athens in 430 BC (Thucydides 2.59), but Sparta had spurned the offer. Now, however, the Athenians in their arrogance assumed they had permanently gained the upper hand and became greedy. The demagogue Cleon, son of Cleaenetus, demanded that the Spartans on the island must first surrender and, further, that Athens be given the cities of Nisaea, Pegae, Troezen and Achaea. The Spartan envoys returned home empty-handed. The arrogance and short-sightedness of the Athenians, especially Cleon, would come back to bite them, although not quite yet.

When the Spartan envoys returned to Pylos, the Athenians refused to return the 60 Spartan triremes, claiming a Spartan violation of the truce. The war was renewed, with the Spartans now at a distinct disadvantage. Athenian ships patrolled the waters off Sphacteria day and night and were now reinforced by 20 more triremes (Thucydides 4.23.2). The Spartans continued their assaults on the fortifications at Pylos; this was actually a poor position, because it had only a small spring and no anchorage for all the Athenian ships, which had to stay on the water. In order to get supplies through to the garrison, Spartan volunteers braved the Athenian blockade in small boats

and by swimming. Helots were offered their freedom if they did likewise and Thucydides relates that many took up the offer (4.26.5–6).

In Athens, there was concern about the straitened circumstances of the Athenian troops, because with winter approaching, it would be impossible to supply them by sea. Cleon, who had led the calls to reject the Spartan offer of peace, was decried; Nicias surrendered his *strategos* command to Cleon, who must, the Assembly insisted, go to Sphacteria and take charge before winter closed in. Cleon – perhaps to hide his apprehension and culpability should he fail – resolved to take no further Athenian troops; he would take only men from Lemnos and Imbros who happened to be in Athens, some peltasts from Aenos (Thucydides 4.28.4) and 400 non-Athenian archers. As his colleague he selected Demosthenes, already in place at Pylos. Cleon claimed he would achieve victory within 20 days.

Meanwhile, a fire had swept across the island of Sphacteria, denuding it of its woods (Thucydides 4.29.2). Thucydides does not relate how many casualties the fire caused. Believing that the fire had effectively removed one feature of the terrain that the Spartans had exploited (the forest in Aetolia had hindered the activities of his men), Demosthenes now saw that the island was easier to navigate than he had first thought. Cleon arrived at Pylos (Thucydides 4.30.4), and with their combined forces, the Athenians prepared to assault the island. First, however, they asked again if the Spartan garrison on the island wished to surrender. The offer was rejected and, a day later, the Athenians launched their assault on Sphacteria. While it was still dark (Thucydides 4.31.1), 800 hoplites were embarked on ships which landed their contingents on both sides of the island at its southern end just before dawn. The hoplites advanced swiftly against the first Spartan guard post on the island. Thucydides relates that this outpost consisted of about 30 hoplites (4.31.2), so this should probably be considered to be a single *enomotia*.

Thucydides breaks off to explain the disposition of the Spartan troops on Sphacteria. In the centre of the island, where the spring was located, was the Spartan camp and the main force. This would have been arranged in a circular formation (Xenophon, *Spartan Constitution* 12.1). A small detachment (*meros*) guarded the heights which looked down on Pylos. An old fort, made in the same fashion as the Athenian fortification at Pylos, was positioned here, but it was not close to a freshwater supply. Spartan forces could, however, retreat to the fort from the camp as a last resort. This detachment must have been less than a full *enomotia* and so fewer than 30 men. In the Spartan camp therefore were probably around 375 hoplites (30 at the guard post and perhaps 15 at the fort) and perhaps approximately 200 helots (adding in some of those who had made it across the waters with supplies).

The guard post at the southern end of the island was immediately overrun (Thucydides 4.32.1), the Athenians charging at full speed and even finding some of the guard still in their beds. The passage of the Athenian ships in the pre-dawn light was presumed simply to be the resumption of the normal patrols. As soon as dawn broke, the rest of the Athenian force disembarked. There were 800 archers and the same number of peltasts and the force included most of the crews of the 70 triremes who had armed themselves. Thucydides notes (4.32.2) that the men of the lowest rowing tier, the *thalamitai*, remained aboard. Per trireme, the lowest tier consisted of 54 men on each of the lowest two banks and 62 on the upper bank; the men of the middle bank were the *zygitai* and those of the upper bank were the *thranitai*. There were also 30 reserve rowers (*perineo*). Therefore, the assault had an additional 146 men per trireme, armed with whatever weaponry they could find: a total of 10,000 men. The Messenians – the ship's crew and 40 hoplites – joined in as well, as did reinforcements from the surrounding area who had decided to side with the Athenians. These reinforcements were divided into two companies, each of around 200 men, which were sent to occupy the highest points on the island to surround the Spartans from all sides and assail them with arrows, javelins, slings and stones (Thucydides 4.32.4).

Epitadas, positioned with the main body of Spartans, saw that the outpost was destroyed and that the full Athenian force was advancing against him. He drew up his hoplites in a line and set out to attack the Athenian hoplites in the centre of the line that was advancing directly towards the Spartans. The lightly armed troops of the Athenians, stationed behind and on the flanks of the hoplites, peppered the much smaller Spartan formation in the flanks with all kinds of missiles, which prevented the Spartan hoplites from closing. The Athenian hoplites did not press their attack, however, because they knew that their overwhelming numbers of missile troops were doing their job. The Spartan hoplites attempted to attack the missile troops who got too bold, but the latter would retreat and then wheel to pepper the enemy with missiles once again (Thucydides 4.33.1–2). The heavily armed Spartan hoplites found it difficult to catch their opponents as the lightly armed Athenians were unarmoured and could scamper away without difficulty.

As the engagement progressed, the Athenian lightly armed troops became more and more bold just as the Spartan defence became less vigorous. Although the Athenians were initially daunted by the thought of sending their hoplites and light infantry against the vaunted Spartans, even when the latter were so substantially outnumbered (Thucydides 4.34.1), this caution disappeared as the battle progressed and the Athenian tactics succeeded. The entire Athenian line charged the Spartans and surrounded them. Thucydides relates (4.34.2) that the shouting of the Athenians as they charged caused

It is rare enough that hoplite shields survive; now in the Museum of the Ancient Agora, Athens, this example of the bronze facing of an *aspis* was actually one of those captured at Pylos in 425 BC and dedicated back in Athens as its inscription relates. Thucydides (4.12.1) mentions Brasidas losing his shield at Pylos as well. (Dorieo/Wikimedia/CC BY-SA 4.0)

consternation among the Spartans, who were accustomed to fighting in near-silence. The ash from the recent fires was also stirred up, adding to the Spartan woes as it obscured their view of the battlefield.

The Spartans closed ranks and retreated to the garrison at the northern end of the island (Thucydides 4.35.1). As soon as the Spartans did so, the Athenian *psiloi* renewed their charge with even louder shouts. Any Spartans who did not remain in formation were killed but the majority reached the fort and took up position there. The Athenians followed the retreat but could not outflank or surround the fort, so they resorted to a frontal assault. The battle raged for most of the day (Thucydides 4.35.3) and the Spartans were able to see off Athenian attacks because they could not be outflanked.

The Messenian *strategos*, Comon – who is only named by Pausanias (4.26.2) – had earlier approached Cleon and Demosthenes with a plan to take some archers and *psiloi* and scale the precipitous northern end of the island to get behind the Spartans in the fort (Thucydides 4.36.1). Comon began the treacherous ascent out of sight. Because the cliff was considered unclimbable, the Spartans had not posted any form of guard. Suddenly appearing on the high ground in the rear of the Spartan position, Comon threw the Spartans into confusion and encouraged those Athenians who saw his emergence. This pragmatic version seems to contradict the Athenians' predetermined plan (Thucydides 4.32.4), however. The climb must have taken a considerable time and it should be assumed that it was planned from the start. Perhaps the Athenians' eventual frontal assault was, in part, to allow the Messenians to get into position unnoticed. Thucydides (4.36.3) compares the state of the Spartans, attacked from both sides, to the final situation of the 300 Spartans at Thermopylae (Herodotus 7.213). Unlike that final last stand, however, where the Spartans died to a man, here, only 50 years later, they surrendered (Thucydides 4.38.1).

Amphipolis

422 BC

BACKGROUND TO BATTLE

The surrender of the Spartan contingent on Sphacteria was a shock – Thucydides calls it the greatest surprise of the war (4.40.1 & 5.14.3), a calamity unlike any Sparta had suffered before. The Spartan envoys had refused even to consider that the garrison might surrender during the peace negotiations. Now, the garrison summoned heralds from the Spartan camp on the mainland who advised them to make their own decision, but to do nothing dishonourable. That warning, no doubt, was intended to dissuade any act of surrender – but they did precisely that. The Spartan force had suffered 30 per cent fatalities; it is not clear how many wounded there were, although it is probable that the vast majority were wounded in some way. Of the original 420 hoplites, 292 surrendered, among them 120 full Spartan citizens (Thucydides 4.38.5). They had endured a 72-day blockade and had survived on what food could be smuggled to the island for 50 of those days. The Spartan *agoge* system inured them to go without, however (Xenophon, *Spartan Constitution* 2.5; Plutarch, *Moralia* 237F/*Spartan Customs* 13). The 292 hoplites were transported back to Athens as prisoners.

This was an unexpected crisis for Sparta. Not only had the Spartan leadership not expected the garrison to surrender and thus sully the honour of all Sparta, but the loss of 120 full citizens was a blow to Spartan manpower that could not be borne and Sparta once again sued for peace. If the calculations made are correct and the original contingent of Spartan citizens was 172 hoplites, Sparta had lost only 50 men, but the loss of 120 more was unbearable (even with the shame of their surrender). It is possible, in light of a later passage (Thucydides 5.15.1), that these were not just any 120 Spartans and that among them were some of the highest-ranking men of the city. This might explain both the Spartan desire for peace (to recover these individuals) and the Athenian unwillingness to agree, although the point is made only once and not clearly. Diodorus also states (12.61.4) that these were the best troops of the Spartans and their allies, but this too is not much to go on.

The Athenians made the threat that if Sparta invaded Attica again, the prisoners would be put to death (Thucydides 4.41.1), but it was expected that the Spartans would negotiate for their release. The Athenians garrisoned Pylos and raids were launched into Laconia from there and the Athenian base at Naupactus. For the Spartans, who had invaded Attica during five of the previous six years, this was an unprecedented taste of their own medicine. Helots began to desert – one of the Spartans' great fears given that they were so outnumbered by their slave population. Sparta sent multiple envoys to negotiate peace and the return of the prisoners from Sphacteria but Athens, flush with confidence and pride, rejected every one of them.

Athenian arrogance was not new, but what is evident in the aftermath of Sphacteria is that it could blind Athens to what was best for the city. Athens certainly had the upper hand, but the Athenians now thought that advantage was permanent and squandered the opportunities it brought. Persuaded by the rhetoric of ambitious (and selfish) demagogues, but also a civic pride which was blind to the dangerous and destructive path being taken, Athens fought on.

At first Athens' confidence was rewarded. The events at Pylos and Sphacteria had begun early in the year's campaigning and the Athenians had also mounted other raids: 80 ships with 2,000 hoplites and 200 cavalry were sent to Corinth, but the Corinthians were ready and waiting. Even so, a closely fought battle at Solygeia ended in Athenian victory (Thucydides 4.43–44); the Corinthians lost 212 men, the Athenians fewer than 50 (Thucydides 4.44.6). Thucydides considers it noteworthy (4.44.5) that the Corinthians were unable to recover two of their dead. Every ancient battle ended in the recovery of the dead and these would be honoured, either on the spot or back in the city. This brief aside indicates the importance placed upon such a ritual.

The Athenians then ravaged Corinthian territory around Crommyon and fortified Methana on their way back to Athens. Sophocles and Eurymedon reached Corcyra and helped the democratic party defeat their oligarchic opposition. They also stood by while the Corcyrean democrats put the opposition to death (Thucydides 4.48.1–6). The Athenians then sailed on to Sicily. In the winter of 425 BC, a Persian envoy, Artaphernes, was captured at Eion on the River Strymon (Thucydides 4.50.1); he was on his way to Sparta, a sign of things to come at the end of the war, which was still 20 years off. The envoy was sent back to Ephesus.

The greatest indication that Athens was squandering its pre-eminence came in the summer of 424 BC when, relatively free from Spartan aggression,

Now in the Antikenmuseen, Berlin (1708), the grave stele of Sosias and Kephisodorus was found at Athens and shows two Athenian hoplites. Each wears a *pilos* helmet, a tunic (*chiton*) and cloak. They shake right hands in the *dexiosis* gesture and carry their shields on the left arm. The left-hand figure also carries his spear butt in his left hand, his shield being held by the *porpax* arm-grip. (Vanni Archive/Getty Images)

the emboldened Athenians pushed too far – not that they would learn their lesson. The campaigning season began with a fleet of 60 Athenian ships and 2,000 hoplites being sent against the island of Cythera off the Laconian coast, which they captured (Thucydides 4.53.1–4). In response, Sparta, having not mounted an invasion of Attica that year, posted garrisons around Laconia, expecting raids from Cythera. Thucydides comments (4.55.2) that in the aftermath of the defeat on Sphacteria, Sparta became more timid than at any time before and lost confidence. On Sicily, a truce was agreed between the Sicilian cities, but when the three Athenian generals (Sophocles, Euymedon and Pythodorus) returned to Athens with this news, they were prosecuted (Thucydides 4.65.3–4) for not subduing all of Sicily on Athens' behalf. Such was the hubris of the Athenians. Athens launched a daring raid to capture Megara (Thucydides 4.67–76) but this was ultimately unsuccessful, thwarted by the actions of Brasidas – who was at Corinth, preparing for his expedition to Thrace (Thucydides 4.74.1). The greatest folly of Athens' overconfidence, however, was to unfold later in the year at Delium.

Immediately after the events at Megara, Demosthenes arrived at Naupactus with 40 ships. He and fellow *strategos* Hippocrates were meddling in Boeotian affairs with a group of democrats who wished to transform their governments and become the allies of Athens rather than Sparta. The Athenians would occupy and fortify Delium, a sanctuary of Apollo in the territory of Tangara, in conjunction with other, simultaneous territory seizures (Thucydides 4.76.1–5) in order to fragment any Boeotian response. When these events occurred in the early winter of 424 BC (Thucydides 4.89.1), the Boeotians gathered in Tangara and were convinced by Pagondas, their principal leader, to attack the Athenians at Delium. Diodorus states (12.69.3) that they had 20,000 infantry and 1,000 cavalry.

In response, Hippocrates levied the entire available forces of Athens (Thucydides 4.90.1), which amounted to 7,000 – the same number of hoplites as the Boeotians, and evidence of the ravages of the plague among the Athenians in 427/426 BC (Thucydides 4.93.3–94.1). Thucydides does not give the other numbers, but there were probably fewer than 1,000 cavalry (300 garrisoned Delium) and the *psiloi* consisted of every available foreigner and poor Athenian – hence Diodorus says (12.69.4) that they outnumbered the Boeotians. The Athenians drew up eight ranks deep but the Thebans – in a sign of what was to come in the 4th century BC – were 25 shields deep, the deepest hoplite phalanx until the battle of Leuctra in 371 BC. The Athenians charged and drove back the Boeotian left (Thucydides 4.96.1–8). On the Boeotian right, however, where the Thebans were, they pushed the Athenians back. Pagondas despatched two squadrons of cavalry to assist the beleaguered left wing (this reserve was another first in hoplite battle – this action is not in Diodorus' account). The arrival of these cavalry threw the troops of the victorious Athenian right wing into a panic, as they thought a new army had arrived; they broke and fled, as did the Athenian left. The routed Athenians were pursued in all directions, losing 1,000 hoplites (and Hippocrates) and countless *psiloi* (Thucydides 4.101.2). The Boeotians lost 500 men. The only positive note for Athens seems to have been the personal bravery in combat of Socrates (Plato, *Symposium* 220D–221C; Plutarch, *Alcibiades* 7.4), but worse was to come.

Before the encounter at Delium, Brasidas had departed for Thrace, taking with him 1,700 hoplites (Thucydides 4.78.1). He marched to Heracleia in Trachis and then through Thessaly and on into Macedonia. Thessaly was pro-Athenian, but Brasidas marched so rapidly that there was no time for the Thessalians to react to his presence. The march and its purpose were uncharacteristic of the newly timid Sparta. Sending an expedition against distant allies of Athens was intended to divert Athenian attention away from raids on the Peloponnese (Thucydides 4.80.1). It also threatened Athens' grain and timber supplies. As Brasidas had shown on multiple occasions previously, he was the perfect

Now in the Louvre (G 458) in Paris, this Attic red-figure cup by the Kodros Painter was created *c*.440–430 BC. It shows Ajax the Lesser abducting Cassandra. The warrior is in typical hoplite garb with *aspis*, *dory*, elaborate helmet and a cloak; note the warrior's shield blazon and the leaf-shaped spearhead and *aspis* of the statue of Athena which Cassandra clutches. (Fine Art Images/Heritage Images/Getty Images)

commander for such a bold and almost un-Spartan undertaking. Brasidas wanted to go and was esteemed at Sparta for his energy (Thucydides 4.81.1). Another advantage for Sparta was that despatching an expedition to such a distant location involved sending helots away from Sparta, thereby removing them from the temptation of revolt sharpened by the proximity of Athenian-occupied Pylos (Thucydides 4.80.3). Thucydides records (4.80.3–4) that 2,000 helots, when asked to announce which of themselves had served Sparta best in war, had been put to death. The story is probably an exaggeration, the kind of story Athenians liked to whisper about the barbarity of Sparta. Nevertheless, Brasidas had with him 700 helot hoplites; accounts of the subsequent fighting at Mantinea refer to these men as *neodomodeis*. He also had Peloponnesian mercenary hoplites. These factors suggest that the Spartan manpower shortage was also a factor in Brasidas' campaign. Most of his men were not Spartan citizens, instead being paid hoplites drawn from other communities in the Peloponnese and, in a remarkable step, helots armed as hoplites. His contingent would become known as the *Brasideioi*.

When Brasidas arrived safely in Thrace, Athens reacted by declaring Perdiccas II, king of Macedonia (r. *c*.448–413 BC), an enemy. Although Perdiccas II intended to ally with Brasidas and campaign against local rivals, Brasidas would not be drawn into local quarrels; he wanted to create allies of Sparta. Brasidas therefore attacked Acanthus in Chalcidice, claiming to bring the 'liberation of Hellas' from Athens (Thucydides 4.85.1). At about the same time as the battle of Delium was being fought, Brasidas conducted an expedition against Amphipolis (Thucydides 4.102.1), the Athenian colony on the River Strymon, marching out from the city of Arnae in Chalcidice and arriving in a snowstorm (Thucydides 4.103.1). Rebels in Amphipolis delivered the bridge over the Strymon to Brasidas and he took the city during the storm, when the small garrison least expected to have to fight.

MAP KEY

1 Cleon advances his force of 1,200 hoplites and allies from Eion to a strong position on the slopes of Mount Pangaion, east of Amphipolis' walls. This movement is intended to reconnoitre the city and plan an attack.

2 As soon as Brasidas observes Cleon's movement from Eion he withdraws his forces from Mount Cerdylium (there to prevent reinforcements reaching Cleon) into Amphipolis. Brasidas selects 150 hoplites (probably Spartan citizens) to be stationed with him at the 'first gate' (**A**); the remainder of his forces are drawn up under Clearidas' command at the Thracian Gate. These include 1,850 hoplites (**B**); 1,000 Chalcidian and Myrcinian peltasts (**C**); 1,500 mercenaries from Thrace (**D**); the cavalry and peltasts of the Edonians (**E**); and 300 cavalry (**F**).

3 Cleon decides to withdraw his forces back towards Eion. He has 1,200 Athenian hoplites, drawn up in ten tribal *taxeis* (**G**), each with approximately 120 men. As *strategos*, Cleon's own *taxis*, of the tribe Pandionis, is probably on the extreme right wing. It is not clear how the other *taxeis* are deployed. Cleon also has 300 cavalry (**H**) as well as allies and the men from Imbros and Lemnos (**I**) on his left wing. Cleon withdraws his left wing first but then, becoming impatient, orders his centre (most of the Athenian *taxeis*) and right wing to withdraw also.

4 Brasidas sees his moment when the centre and right wing of the Athenians begin withdrawing. He charges his select hoplites out of the 'first gate' into the retreating Athenian centre. The Athenian left wing hurries back to Eion. Although outnumbered, Brasidas' well-ordered force charges the retreating centre, the warriors of which have their right sides exposed, and throws them into disarray.

5 Clearidas leads the remainder of the Spartan forces out of the Thracian Gate against the Athenian right wing, and to reinforce Brasidas against the centre. Cleon flees and is cut down. The right wing withdraws to its starting position on high ground.

6 Brasidas is mortally wounded in the Athenian centre, but is carried from the field alive. The Athenian centre suffers heavy casualties.

7 The Athenian right withstands several of Clearidas' charges but, surrounded by cavalry as well as peltasts hurling missiles, the Athenians withdraw with difficulty to Eion.

Battlefield environment

The hills in front of the fortifications of Amphipolis offered a commanding view down on to the site of the walls of the city, situated on a low plateau in a bend of the River Strymon. Likewise, the view from the Acropolis of Amphipolis offered commanding views of the surrounding hills, just as Thucydides relates (5.7.3–5). Across the river and commanding the site of the bridge, Mount Cerdylium (the modern St Catherine's Hill, with an elevation of 152m) gives views across the Strymon towards both Eion and Amphipolis. The Athenians took up position on the lower slopes of Pangaion, on the east side opposite the 'long walls' of Amphipolis (Thucydides 4.102.4). These walls ran roughly north–south across most of the bend in the Strymon parallel to the modern road (which runs along the line of the ancient road) and then turned westwards towards the bridge. The road to Eion (4.5km to the south) ran away from the Athenian position to the south-east. The 'first gate' was located close to the angle of the turn in the south-eastern corner of the wall and on the eastern edge of the plateau. This allowed Brasidas' small force to run from the gate and reach the retreating Athenian centre. The Thracian Gate, through which the main body of Spartan and allied troops would charge under Clearidas, was located north of the initial Athenian position and gave access to the north–south road.

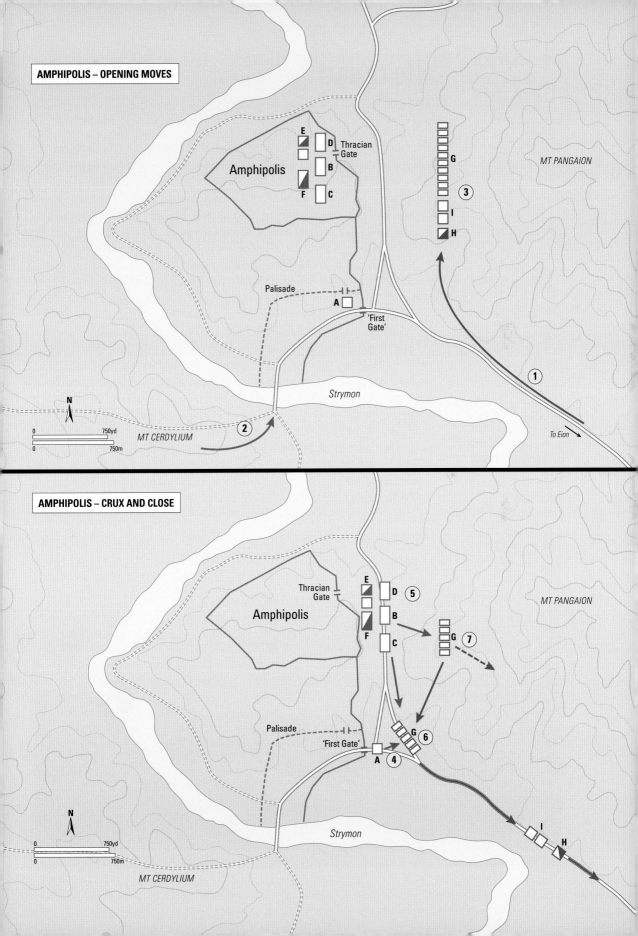

AMPHIPOLIS – OPENING MOVES

Amphipolis

E
D — Thracian Gate
B
F
C

G
③
I
H

Palisade
A
'First Gate'

N

Strymon

0   750yd
0   750m

MT CERDYLIUM

②

①

To Eion

MT PANGAION

AMPHIPOLIS – CRUX AND CLOSE

E — Thracian Gate
D   ⑤
B
F
C

G   ⑦

Amphipolis

G   ⑥

Palisade
'First Gate'
A   ④

N

Strymon

0   750yd
0   750m

MT CERDYLIUM

I
H

MT PANGAION

INTO COMBAT

Brasidas did not immediately take the city itself, however, but instead plundered the area; the defenders, including the Athenian general Eucles, were able to close the town to him. The historian Thucydides was the other Athenian commander in the area, based at the island of Thasos, 80km or half a day's sail from Amphipolis. Eucles sent for him and he departed with seven ships for Amphipolis – or at least to secure Eion, at the mouth of the Strymon, 25 stadia (4.5km) from Amphipolis (Thucydides 4.104.4–5). Thucydides' own involvement in this campaign might make his information seem reliable, but he may have distorted his account to favour the part he played, especially since he was exiled from Athens for his perceived lack of action. Brasidas, aware of Thucydides' imminent arrival, offered reasonable terms – any residents who stayed would be allowed to keep their property and he gave five days' amnesty for anyone to leave. The city therefore capitulated to Brasidas, on the same day as Thucydides reached Eion (Thucydides 4.106.3). Owing to this success, other towns came over to Brasidas as well.

The capture of Amphipolis alarmed Athens and Brasidas' reasonable conduct suddenly made him (and Sparta) an attractive ally for the cities of the area. Mass revolt among Athens' allies in the region was now a very real possibility. What was more, Athens had just suffered a humiliating defeat and was considered to be geographically remote (the resilience of Athens was something they and the Spartans underestimated). Later that year, Athens could do little but did manage to send out additional garrisons to some of the cities in the area (Thucydides 4.108.6). Brasidas, meanwhile, sent news of his success back to Sparta and requested reinforcements of his own. These were not forthcoming, according to Thucydides (4.108.6–7), because the Spartans were still preoccupied

This image of Casta Hill, a burial mound found north of Amphipolis, shows how commanding a view the hills which surround it had into the city. Cleon sought to take advantage of this by advancing to Mount Pangaion. As can be appreciated, however, Brasidas could also clearly see the position of the Athenians and when they chose to move off. (Athanasios Gioumpasis/ Getty Images)

with the recovery of the prisoners taken on Sphacteria, and Brasidas only had a few Spartans with him. Brasidas did not remain idle, however. He conquered most of the area of Acte around Mount Athos and took the Athenian city of Torone on the Sithonian peninsula.

In the spring of 423 BC, the Athenians and Spartans agreed to a truce lasting for a year (Thucydides 4.117.1; the terms are given at 4.118.1–11). This would run from roughly the end of March until the same time the following year, which corresponded to the 14th day of the Athenian month Elaphebolion and probably the 12th day of the Spartan month Gerastius. Such was the danger of Brasidas' success that Athens' refusal to entertain peace proposals was, though not overturned, certainly diminished. The truce would prevent Brasidas from further conquest and the recruitment of any more allies against Athens and the Athenians could make preparations to dislodge him. The Spartans tried yet again to recover the prisoners taken on Sphacteria. During the truce, envoys attempted to negotiate peace without luck.

Before news of the truce had reached Thrace, allies of Athens such as the city of Scione, went over to Brasidas, crowning him as a liberator of Hellas (Thucydides 4.121.1). Brasidas was also planning to take Potidaea and Mende when news of the truce came. Disagreement over the timing of the revolt of Scione almost broke the truce. In Athens, in another dangerous sign, Cleon proposed a motion – which the assembly passed – for the destruction of Scione and the execution of the city's entire male population. Brasidas was firm in maintaining that Scione was a Spartan ally and this encouraged other towns to revolt. Mende went over to Sparta (Thucydides 4.123.1) and Athens turned its wrath on them too. Brasidas evacuated the women and children from both cities in preparation for the Athenian response, which he predicted would come in the following year. He also allied with Perdiccas II again, this time defeating his Macedonian rival, Arrhabaeus. Illyrian allies changed sides and Brasidas found himself retreating, forced to face Arrhabaeus alone deep within hostile territory, and without local guides because Perdiccas II's army had melted away.

ABOVE LEFT
Although termed 'heavy' infantry by modern commentators, hoplites were capable of moving swiftly if required. This terracotta *pinax* (votive tablet) dating from *c*.520 BC and now in the Acropolis Museum, Athens, shows a running hoplite. The position of the shield and underarm spear hold are noteworthy, as is the cloak tied around the waist. The original name has been erased but *kalos* ('beautiful') remains. (DEA/G. NIMATALLAH/De Agostini via Getty Images)

ABOVE RIGHT
This Attic *krater* found in Pharsala, southern Thessaly, and dating from *c*.530 BC, shows both the widespread nature of Attic art and the continuity of hoplite battle. Here the helmet, *dory* and *aspides* are obvious, as is the stance of the hoplites. The bronze cuirass and greaves give away the earlier date. Note the interior shield grip and the shield blazons which include a *triskeles*, a three-legged design. (Prisma/UIG/ Getty Images)

Cleon

The Athenian aristocrat Cleon first came to prominence at the outbreak of the Peloponnesian War. He was the voice of the 'war party', who favoured fighting the Spartans when they invaded Attica. He also led the calls for Pericles to be prosecuted. With the death of Pericles in 429 BC, Cleon's voice became dominant and he was lambasted by both Aristophanes and Thucydides.

Cleon became the first demagogue, a forceful and charismatic speaker, and persuaded the Athenian *demos* to follow his ideas. Although he lacked the eloquence of Pericles, his voice was usually heeded. Cleon also led vicious attacks on his opponents. It was he who proposed putting the entire male population of Mytilene to death in 427 BC. The Athenian *demos* agreed and despatched a ship. The following day, cooler heads prevailed and a fast ship carrying an instruction reversing the decision was sent to catch the first ship (which it did).

It was Cleon who led the calls to reject the Spartan peace proposals in 425 BC and his hand was then forced – by Nicias, the leader of those keen to make peace if it was on offer – to put an army into the field himself to win on the island of Sphacteria. Other than his own training as a hoplite, it is not clear whether Cleon possessed any military acumen, but he was given command of the Athenian forces that reinforced Demosthenes on Sphacteria. What is certain is that it was Demosthenes who devised the Athenian strategy that proved successful on Sphacteria, but Cleon was able to bask in the glory.

Cleon was impatient to be given the command of the Athenian troops operating against Amphipolis in 422 BC and as soon as the truce of 423 BC expired he made his way from Athens. His capture of the city of Torone shows that he possessed some military skill, but he undid all of that by his reckless and disastrous conduct at Amphipolis. Having imperilled his force there, retreating within reach of an enemy force, he panicked and fled and was cut down by a lowly peltast. Half of his warriors were killed.

Brasidas retreated with his hoplites in a hollow square formation, the lightly armed troops in the centre (Thucydides 4.125.2–4). He placed his youngest troops in the front lines so they could dash out against the enemy if required and he selected 300 men to act as a rearguard against enemy attacks. The tactic worked and Brasidas' force continued to repulse enemy attacks as they retreated (Thucydides 4.127.1). Arrhabaeus set an ambush on two hills along the road he knew Brasidas must take to leave his territory. Brasidas foresaw this and despatched his 300 picked troops to charge the ambushing force on one of the hills before the rest of Arrhabaeus' troops could encircle them. This picked Spartan force dislodged the enemy from the hill allowing Brasidas' contingent to make easier progress through the ambush site. Reaching Perdiccas II's territory, Brasidas' forces treated the Macedonian king's subjects as hostile and the king thereafter regarded Brasidas as an enemy.

Returning from Macedonia, Brasidas discovered that an Athenian force was already in occupation of Mende. The Athenians had sailed against Scione and Mende with 50 ships and 1,000 hoplites, 600 archers, 1,000 Thracian mercenaries and an unrecorded number of peltasts (Thucydides 4.129.2). The Athenian generals, Nicias and Nicostratus, had based themselves at Potidaea, Athens' hard-won spoil after a three-year siege (432–429 BC). The Athenian force advanced against Mende and was met by 300 Scionaeans, 700 Peloponnesian hoplites led by Polydamidas and the men of Mende. Nicias attacked uphill with 120 *psiloi*, 60 picked hoplites and all of his 600 archers, but was unable to dislodge the enemy. Nicostratus, at the head of the remaining Athenian troops, took a longer, more difficult route; he lost his way, however, and the Athenians narrowly avoided destruction (Thucydides 4.129.4–5). Mende was betrayed to the Athenians the following day, but they

Brasidas was the son of Tellis and Argileonis. His mother is prominent in the literary tradition, associated with the pithy sayings of Spartan mothers. Brasidas first appears in 431 BC during the siege of Methone, where he led 100 hoplites on a dash through the scattered Athenian besiegers and became the first Spartan honoured during the Peloponnesian War. This bold manoeuvre and the use of a select force was something he would repeat.

In 430 BC Brasidas led a daring raid on the unprotected Piraeus from Megara, having surprised the Athenians by marching his ships' crews from Corinth. In 429 BC he was the eponymous *ephoros* at Sparta (Xenophon, *Hellenica* 2.3.10), suggesting that he was already well over 30. Brasidas again showed his personal bravery at Pylos in 425 BC, leading his ship to attack the Athenian position, but he fainted due to the number of wounds he had sustained. He lost his shield, and perhaps the surviving Spartan shield taken from Pylos and dedicated in the Athenian *agora* was his.

In 424 BC he mustered a force at Corinth to take to Thrace – another farsighted strategy for the usually inward-looking Spartans. When Athens attacked Megara, Brasidas led a detachment of his forces at Corinth and thwarted the Athenian siege. Brasidas then showed he had more than one string to his bow by making his way through treacherous Thessaly by a series of rapid marches, thus avoiding trouble. In Thrace, he persuaded several cities to join Sparta without bloodshed, instead convincing them that Sparta would be a better, and more moderate, master than Athens. He also showed himself a master of retreat when withdrawing from hostile territory in Macedonia.

Brasidas met his death at Amphipolis in 422 BC leading a daring charge of 150 hoplites against the retreating Athenian centre. Even though he was one of only seven recorded Spartan casualties, his tactic was an overwhelming success and he inflicted a humiliating defeat on Athens.

plundered it; the 700 Peloponnesian hoplites took refuge on the acropolis, and eventually made their way to Scione. The Athenians turned on Scione with a circumvallation and Perdiccas II sent word that he wished to ally with them against Brasidas (Thucydides 4.132.1).

Despite Sparta's senior leadership deciding (partly owing to jealousy of Brasidas) not to send reinforcements, they did send a group to investigate how Brasidas was progressing. This group consisted of Ischagoras, Ameinias and Aristaeus but they were bringing an army. Contrary to custom, they brought young Spartans with them (Thucydides 4.132.3), perhaps men disaffected by the new timidity and inaction at Sparta. Before winter was over, Brasidas, in a characteristically bold move, made an attempt on Potidaea but was unsuccessful (Thucydides 4.135.1).

As soon as the year-long truce expired in 422 BC, Cleon persuaded the Athenians to choose him to lead an expedition to Thrace with 1,200 hoplites and 300 cavalry, larger numbers of allies and 30 ships (Thucydides 5.2.1). Athens had only 6,000 citizen hoplites to call upon after Delium, so this undertaking represented 20 per cent of its total resources. The force landed at Scione, which was still under siege; taking some of the besieging force, Cleon moved towards Cophus, close to the city of Torone and held by Brasidas' forces. The Spartan garrison was unable to defend Torone against the Athenian assault and the city fell to Cleon. Brasidas, who was on his way to relieve Torone, retreated to Amphipolis.

Cleon embarked on his ships and sailed for Amphipolis. He based himself at Eion (Thucydides 5.6.1) and was successful in taking several of the cities which had gone over to Brasidas. Cleon also summoned allied troops from both Perdiccas II and Thrace. To counter this, Brasidas encamped on Mount Cerdylium to block the reinforcements' approach. From there,

Brasidas could observe the reinforcements and also the movements of Cleon's forces from Eion. Brasidas also called upon reinforcements from local allies and received 1,500 Thracian mercenaries, 1,000 Chalcidian and Myrcinian peltasts and all the troops of the Edonians (cavalry and peltasts) (Thucydides 5.6.3–4). He had, in total, 2,000 hoplites and 300 Greek cavalry, 1,500 of whom he took to Mount Cerdylium while the remainder stayed in Amphipolis under his second-in-command, Clearidas.

In the face of this Spartan activity, Cleon seems to have remained inactive and, given the fickle nature of the Athenian *demos*, his soldiers began questioning whether he was best suited to command. Cleon may still have been awaiting reinforcements, but these rumours of disquiet made him move his forces to a strong (*karteros*) position on a hill to the east of Amphipolis' walls (Thucydides 5.7.4). This was probably an outrunner of Mount Pangaion, 140m high and directly opposite the wall (and subsequently the site of a Macedonian tomb). Thucydides relates (5.7.3) that this was a reconnaissance, but Cleon may have been playing into Brasidas' hands and exposing his troops to attack. Whatever Cleon's expectation of reinforcements, none seem to have been despatched from Athens and any from Perdiccas II or Thrace did not reach him (Thucydides mentions the belated Spartan reinforcements at 5.12–13). Diodorus' picture is very different. He comments (12.73.3) that Cleon needed to launch successive assaults on Eion, suggesting that Thucydides himself may not have secured the port.

As soon as Brasidas observed the movement from the Athenian camp, he moved his troops back into Amphipolis. Thucydides relates (5.8.1–2) that Brasidas did not trust the quality of his troops against the Athenians, who also had the pick of the troops from Lemnos and Imbros, but this seems unlikely. Brasidas duly selected 150 hoplites (5.8.4) and assigned the rest to Clearidas. It is conceivable that these 150 were Spartan *homoioi* just as Brasidas' picked force at Methone had been in 431 BC (Thucydides 2.25.2); he could rely on their discipline and ability to stay in formation, their bravery and their perseverance. It is possible that Brasidas intended to use these 150 as some kind of bait or as a holding force, which would match the bold stratagems he had undertaken in the past. With these 150 hoplites, he intended to attack before the Athenians could fully withdraw (Thucydides 5.8.4–5) and allow the rest of his troops to sally forth from the Thracian Gate. From his position on Mount Cerdylium, Brasidas had a commanding view of the Amphipolis battlefield and he may well have devised his stratagem there and then. He instructed Clearidas to take up position at the Thracian Gate with the remainder of their forces (Thucydides 5.10.1).

One reason for the selection of so small a force may be explained by the fact that, from Cleon's position on the hill, the Athenian commander could see the entire Spartan contingent behind the walls and count the number of men and horses (Thucydides 5.10.2). When Cleon approached closer, he could see the Spartan force, and decided that he could easily withdraw before they could attack him. Therefore, the retreat was sounded and the Athenian force turned to take the road back to Eion on their left. This process was probably undertaken starting with the left wing; based on the account of Herodotus

(6.111), Cleon himself would have been stationed on the right wing. Cleon became impatient with how long this manoeuvre was taking, however, and he wheeled his right wing towards the left, exposing their unshielded right sides to the Spartans (Thucydides 5.10.4). At this moment, Brasidas seized his opportunity and charged his small force at the retreating Athenians.

The speech given to Brasidas by Thucydides (5.10.5–6) is revealing. He encouraged his soldiers by stating that he could tell the Athenians were retreating by the way their spears moved. The small force charged out of the 'first gate' and made its way along the road towards the retreating Athenians, hitting the Athenian centre; Cleon's men were panicked and shocked at such audacity. At the same moment, Clearidas exited the Thracian Gate with the remainder of the Spartan army and bore down on the Athenians.

It is possible that Brasidas had already taken his small force out towards the Athenians, and that this prompted Cleon's retreat (or his impatience). It would seem unlikely that this small force could charge a great distance and panic the Athenians, however, so it is possible that they were already en route and Brasidas expected them to be ignored because of their modest numbers, or he had seen a way for them to remain undetected. He must have been sure they could fight for long enough in order to allow Clearidas to reach the remainder of the Athenians. A stratagem recorded in Frontinus (1.5.23) – that Brasidas allowed himself to be enveloped and then broke through the thinned Athenian line – seems unbelievable. This stratagem – and another in Polyaenus (1.38.2) – may also relate to an entirely different action, but not one recorded by Thucydides or Diodorus.

Whatever the specifics of these manoeuvres, Brasidas' compact force wreaked havoc among the troops of the retreating Athenian centre, who had not expected any attack and were quickly routed. The Athenian left wing, closest to Eion already, fled back to the port. At this moment, pressing his attack in the Athenian centre, Brasidas was wounded – but the Athenians

Brasidas charges the Athenians

Cleon has ordered the Athenian phalanx consisting of 1,200 hoplites to withdraw from its commanding position on Mount Pangaion, facing the long walls of Amphipolis. The men of the left wing have already turned to their left and withdrawn some way back towards the Athenian camp at Eion, 4.5km to the south. Impatient to withdraw more quickly, Cleon has ordered both the Athenian centre and the Athenian right to withdraw as well. Both divisions have turned, exposing their unshielded right sides to the Spartans in Amphipolis.

Seeing that the Athenian withdrawal is beginning, inside Amphipolis Brasidas has chosen 150 hoplites, perhaps five *enomotiai* of Spartans. When the Athenian centre is on the road back to Eion, Brasidas chooses his moment and charges his select force out of the 'first gate', along the road and into the exposed right flank of the Athenian centre. Not expecting to be charged, and certainly not by so small a force, the hoplites of the Athenian centre do not have enough time to react and are without leadership.

Along with Aristophanes and Cratinus, Eupolis of Athens was one of the founders of the 'Old Comedy'. Eupolis' entire career took place within the Peloponnesian War and he probably took up arms as a hoplite from 428 BC. Later he served as a rower and died in c.411 BC, possibly at the battle of Cynossema. Like Aristophanes, Eupolis criticized contemporary Athenian commanders such as Alcibiades, Callias, Phormion and Hyperbolus over their conduct of the war. Eupolis also pointed out abuses, such as unqualified men being elected as generals. Alas, no full play of Eupolis' survives and only fragments remain. This bust, found in 1998, finally put a face to a figure who was until then only a name. (Timoleon75/Wikimedia/CC BY-SA 4.0)

did not realize it. The Athenian right wing stood its ground. Cleon fled as soon as the first attack came and was cut down by a Myrcinian peltast (Thucydides 5.10.9; a detail probably intended to suggest ignominy). Clearidas attacked the Athenian right wing, still on the hill, but it repulsed three of his charges. Only when surrounded by peltasts and harassed by cavalry did the Athenians on the right break, small detachments taking difficult and circuitous routes back to Eion. Along the way they were picked off by cavalry or peltasts (Thucydides 5.10.9–10).

Brasidas was carried from the field, still alive, back into the city. There he learned of his victory before succumbing to his wounds (Thucydides 5.10.11). He was subsequently given a public burial and honoured as a hero and founder at Amphipolis, supplanting the previous hero, the Athenian Hagnon, who had founded the city in 437/436 BC. The casualties were notably one-sided, according to Thucydides (5.11.2): the Athenians suffered 600 dead – 10 per cent of Athens' total available hoplite forces in 422 BC – while Brasidas' forces lost only seven men.

Again, the account of Diodorus is very different and cannot be reconciled with that of Thucydides. Diodorus states (12.74.1–2) that, from his assaults on Eion, Cleon marched against Brasidas in Amphipolis and that Brasidas drew up his army and marched out against Cleon. Diodorus' account of the battle is stereotypical and not much help – he comments that it was fierce and evenly balanced at first, but fell into confusion because both leaders were slain in battle and the Spartans emerged victorious. There is none of the detail given by Thucydides, although it is noteworthy that Diodorus gives Cleon a brave death, similar to Brasidas', which may make his account seem less reliable to some.

According to Thucydides (5.11.3), the Athenians sailed back to Athens, leaving Clearidas as master of Amphipolis. A contingent of 900 Spartan hoplite reinforcements had reached Heracleia in Trachis en route to assist Brasidas when the battle was fought, and they learned of his death in Thessaly, at which point they returned home (Thucydides 5.12.1).

With Brasidas' death, Sparta had lost one of its most energetic and inspired commanders; it would take some time for a new, dynamic leader to emerge. In losing Cleon, Athens had not really suffered a notable setback; his death allowed new demagogues to emerge, but they followed the same self-

The silver ossuary with gold crown, discovered in the *agora* of Amphipolis, was found at the spot where Brasidas was reportedly buried as a hero. It has therefore been identified with Brasidas and is now in the Archaeological Museum of Amphipolis. (Rjdeadly/Wikimedia/CC BY-SA 4.0)

aggrandizing and ambitious pattern he had displayed, and offered the same kind of threat to Athens. Nevertheless, the defeat at Amphipolis, coming as it did on the heels of the defeat at Delium, meant that Athens was finally forced to agree to peace (Thucydides 5.14.1). Cleon had, of course, been the Athenian politician most opposed to peace, as Brasidas had been on the Spartan side (Thucydides 5.16.1). Sparta remained desperate to recover its citizens taken prisoner at Sphacteria.

For Sparta it was King Pleistoanax (r. 458–409 BC), Agis II's co-ruler, who now urged peace and for Athens, Nicias, one of Athens' most successful generals. The terms of their agreement, the Peace of Nicias, signed in early 421 BC (Thucydides 5.18–19), were intended to last 50 years (Thucydides 5.18.3). Cities taken by each side were to be restored and several were to have their independence guaranteed. Most importantly for the Spartans, the prisoners from Sphacteria (and other engagements) would be returned (Thucydides 5.18.7).

Mantinea

418 BC

BACKGROUND TO BATTLE

The Peace of Nicias in 421 BC was supposed to last 50 years. Once again, however, Athens squandered the advantages of peace by allying with Sparta's enemies in the Peloponnese, namely Argos, Elis and Mantinea. Mantinea was determined to maintain the freedom from Sparta it had attained (Thucydides 5.69.1) and the cities of Argolis were determined to reassert their influence in the region, lost especially since the Persian Wars. Elis had humiliated Sparta at the Olympian Games in July 420 BC (Thucydides 5.49–50), claiming that Sparta had breached the Olympic truce and taken the Elean city of Lepreum. According to Thucydides (5.55.1), the alliance was made at Athens' instigation. According to Plutarch (*Alcibiades* 15.1), it was Alcibiades who brought the Athenians into alliance with the Mantineans and it was he who when appointed general (probably in 420 BC) was despatched with a force of 1,000 hoplites. Not needed, this force returned home to Athens.

An additional Athenian garrison of 300 men was then sent to aid Argos at Epidaurus (Thucydides 5.56.1–2). Argos had invaded Epidaurus and put it under siege; Agis II sent a large army to oppose the Argives (the same force that would take the field at Mantinea), but did not fight. When battle was refused, the Athenians had not yet joined the alliance that year; the troops were still marching out with their new commanders. Agis II eventually secured a four-month peace (Thucydides 5.60.1) although he agreed to this without consulting any Spartan magistrate as he should have done. The disgruntled Spartan troops withdrew to their homes.

Likewise, the Argives stoned Thrasyllus, their general; he had proposed peace, but fled to an altar for sanctuary. The arrival of the Athenian contingent (Thucydides 5.61.1) spurred the alliance back into action and the Athenians rejected a peace about which they had not been consulted. Despite the recent peace, the alliance forces now moved on the Arcadian town of Orchomenos, which was put under siege; it capitulated quickly. According to Thucydides (5.61.1), the Athenian contingent was commanded by Laches and Nicostratus and it is possible that one man commanded the infantry while the other commanded the *hippeis*. The sources explain that Alcibiades had originally commanded the 1,000 hoplites and Agesippidas the garrison of 300, so these new commanders were presumably their normal, annually elected replacements. The members of the alliance were divided as to whether to proceed against Tegea as the Mantineans wished, or against Lepreum, as proposed by the Eleans (Thucydides 5.62.1–2). The commanders from both Argos and Athens sided with Mantinea and opted to proceed against Tegea, which prompted the Eleans to return home with their 3,000 hoplites.

Despite bringing his army – the finest Greece had yet seen (Thucydides 5.60.3) – into the field, Agis II had avoided battle. When news of the fall of Orchomenos was received, the Spartans decided that they would fine their king and raze his house (Thucydides 5.63.2). When Agis II promised to wipe out the stain on his honour, the Spartans relented but the Spartan council of elders, the Gerousia, censured the king and appointed ten overseers (*xymbouloi*) to keep an eye on his performance. Agis II could take no action without their approval – an unprecedented curtailing of a king's power. With the permission of the ten overseers, which the king now needed in order to act, the Spartan army marched on Tegea in full force and with helots in support, having been told that unless they came, Tegea would be forced to go over to the Athenian alliance. At Maenalia the Spartans summoned their Arcadian allies, sent home one-sixth of the Spartan force – the older and younger men, probably numbering 700 – to guard Sparta and advanced on Tegea, then invaded the territory of Mantinea.

The men of Mantinea, the Athenians and their allies drew up for battle on a steep hill. The Spartans were almost tempted into attacking uphill and got within javelin range (Thucydides 5.65.2). Perhaps the king was too keen to make amends, but Agis II now had second thoughts. Instead, the Spartans withdrew towards Tegea, south of Mantinea, and there diverted the course of a stream into Mantinean territory, thereby damaging the land, in order to lure the troops of the alliance down from their commanding position to fight a battle on the plain.

Thucydides reports (5.65.5) that the Athenians and their allies were amazed that the Spartans had advanced towards them, uphill, getting to within a javelin cast before stopping, turning about and retreating down the hill out of sight. The leaders of the alliance thought that they had, once again, lost the opportunity for a decisive fight. The Spartan plan succeeded, however, and the Athenians and their allies advanced onto the plain and spent the night there, intent on pursuing what they thought were the retreating Spartans. The Spartans, meanwhile, moved from the stream to the precinct of Heracles where their camp was situated (Thucydides 5.64.5 & 5.66.1). The Athenians and their allies formed up for battle in the morning and advanced, ready to fight at a moment's notice.

This funerary stele of Panaitios from Athens, *c.*400 BC, shows an unarmoured cavalryman. Note the size of the horse, which is much smaller than modern breeds. Athens had the advantage that if it was to lose while opposing Sparta in the Peloponnese, Athenian forces were not fighting on home soil but were providing a real threat to Spartan hegemony. One might ask therefore why Athens sent only 1,000 hoplites and 300 cavalry (*hippeis*) to Mantinea. Actually, in 418 BC, 1,000 was a much greater proportion of Athens' available manpower than earlier in the Peloponnesian War. At Delium Athens only had 7,000 hoplites to call upon and lost 1,000 of them. At Amphipolis the Athenian force lost 600 more and so Athens' full contingent was now only 5,400, which meant that the 1,000 hoplites at Mantinea represented almost 20 per cent of Athens' available manpower. The 300 *hippeis* were probably the garrison sent to Epidaurus (although not described as cavalry earlier – this may have had interesting ramifications). Some of the Athenians were colonists from Aegina (Thucydides 5.74.2). (Prisma/ UIG/Getty Images)

MAP KEY

1 The allied army of Mantineans, Arcadians and Athenians advances south from its secure position on the slopes near Mantinea in order to catch the Spartan and Peloponnesian army, which has withdrawn towards Tegea. Camping on the plain in formation, the allied forces continue their advance in the early morning. The Spartans are encamped just north of Pelagos Wood in the Sanctuary of Heracles. The allies advance in battle order. On the right flank is the Mantinean contingent (**A**), followed by the Arcadian hoplites (**B**). Next to them are the 1,000 picked Argives (**C**), then the remainder of the men of Argos, the *pentelochoi* (**D**); then the men of Cleonae and Orneae (**E**); and next to them, the 1,000-man Athenian contingent is drawn up in its usual ten tribal *taxeis*, with 100 men per *taxis* (**F**). Laches, the *strategos*, was from the tribe of Cecropis so his *taxis* is stationed on the right; the order of the remaining nine *taxeis* is not known. On the extreme left of the Athenian line are 300 cavalry (**G**).

2 Although surprised by the arrival of the Athenians and their allies, the Spartans recover and deploy quickly. The Spartan army includes a contingent of Spartan cavalry (**H**); a small contingent of Spartans, commanded by the *polemarchoi* Hipponoïdas and Aristocles (**I**); the contingent of Tegea (**J**); the Maenalians (**K**); the Heraeans (**L**); and the Spartan contingent itself (**M**), composed of five *lochoi*, each 512 men strong, with King Agis II and his 300-strong *hippeis* bodyguard in the centre. Next to the leftmost Spartan *lochoi* is a *lochos* of freed helots, the *neodamodeis* (**N**); a *lochos* of Brasidas' veterans, the *Brasideioi* (**O**), is to their left. On the extreme left is a 600-strong unit of lightly armed *Skiritai* (**P**) and a contingent of Spartan cavalry (**Q**).

3 After preliminary speeches and prayers to the gods, the armies advance, both edging to the right as they do so. The Mantinean and Arcadian right extends beyond the Spartan left, and the Spartan right extends beyond the Athenians on the allied left.

4 Agis II realizes that his left is in danger of being outflanked. He orders the *Skiritai*, *Brasideioi* and *neodamodeis* to move further to the left and extend the line as far as the Mantinean line. This creates a gap in the Spartan line between the three *lochoi* now on the extreme left and the leftmost Spartan *lochos*. Agis orders his *polemarchoi* from the right wing to fill this gap with two *lochoi*; the *polemarchoi* refuse. Too late, Agis II orders the *Skiritai* to fill the gap, but by now the Mantineans, Arcadians and the picked Argives have taken advantage of the gap in the line.

5 The Mantineans and Arcadians engage with the *neodamodeis*, *Brasideioi* and *Skiritai*, pushing them back. The picked Argives rush into the gap and threaten to envelop the left of the Spartan line.

6 The remainder of the Spartan and allied lines continue to advance. The Spartan right threatens to envelop the Athenian left but is prevented from doing so by the brave actions of the Athenian cavalry.

7 The Spartan *lochoi* reach the Athenians and other allied troops, quickly routing them. The Athenian cavalry prevent the rout from being worse.

8 The Spartans wheel their line to fight the victorious picked Argives, Mantineans and Arcadians. The Spartans surround them but allow the enemy to flee rather than force them to fight to the finish.

Battlefield environment

The battlefield of Mantinea was ground of the Spartans' choosing. They had wanted to lure the allied army away from its commanding position on the heights; Thucydides (5.65.1) relates that the terrain there was steep and difficult to access. This was most likely the hill situated to the north of Mantinea, although others place the initial allied position at Mount Alesion, to the east of Mantinea. Either way, this spot had no part to play in the actual battle.

The remainder of the terrain was a flat, gently undulating plain, the perfect battlefield for hoplite phalanxes to fight upon – this is why at least three decisive battles were fought at Mantinea in the 5th and 4th centuries BC. The town of Mantinea itself was destroyed by the Spartans in 385 BC and, although rebuilt, there has been little urban build-up in the millennia since. To prompt the allied forces' unlikely move away from a position of great strength, the Spartans advanced up the hill very close to the allied army before turning and retreating. They then withdrew and flooded the plain by diverting the course of a stream in Tegean territory. This was either the stream today known as Sarandapotamos or, more likely, the Zanovistas, which flowed north from it into Mantinean territory. The former is a larger watercourse, the latter is in the better position.

The allied commanders thought that they had missed their opportunity and advanced onto the plain, south of Mantinea itself, spending the night there and advancing in the morning in formation. No mention is made of Pelagos Wood, 5km south of Mantinea, so the battle should be situated further north of it. Indeed, the Sanctuary of Heracles in which the Spartans camped (Thucydides 5.64.5 & 5.66.1) was on the northern edge of the wood. The Spartans seem to have been surprised that their trick worked so well; they advanced beyond the flooded part of the plain and prepared to face the allied army advancing to meet them in formation.

MANTINEA – OPENING MOVES

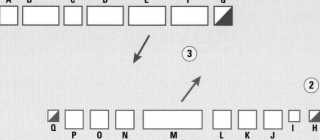

A B C D E F G

Q P O N M L K J I H

1 2 3

Sanctuary
of Heracles

**Spartan
camp**

N

0 ——— 500yd
0 ——— 500m

PELAGOS WOOD

MANTINEA – CRUX AND CLOSE

A B C D E F G

8 7 5

Q P O N M L K J I H

6 4

Sanctuary
of Heracles

**Spartan
camp**

N

0 ——— 500yd
0 ——— 500m

PELAGOS WOOD

INTO COMBAT

Thucydides' description of the deployment of the Spartan line at Mantinea is one of the most remarkable in ancient warfare. First, he gives a breakdown of the Spartan chain of command which is one of the most detailed that survives (there are a few issues with other sources, but it is remarkably cohesive). Thucydides states (5.66.2–4) that Agis II directed the movement of each contingent of the army – as the law prescribed – and then goes into detail, perhaps for readers who were not familiar with Spartan systems. The king gave his orders to the *polemarchoi* and they passed them to the commanders of the Spartan *lochoi, the lochagoi*. They then gave the orders to the *pentekonteres*, the commanders of the *pentekostyes*, the 'fiftieths', and they in turn transmitted them to the commanders of the *enomotiai*, the *enomotarchoi*, each of whom then gave the commands to his *enomotia*. Some would have the *polemarchoi* as the commanders of the six *morae* mentioned later in the war by Xenophon (*Hellenica* 2.4.31), but Thucydides never uses the term. Thucydides admired this chain of command, as it had a clear line for orders to pass along, and responsibility devolved upon many. Thucydides reports (5.66.2) that when they Spartans spotted the allied forces advancing in battle order, they were surprised, and had never been in such consternation. Owing to the quality of their command structure, however, the Spartans were able to deploy quickly.

The five *lochoi* of the Spartan Obal army were augmented with another *lochos* composed of *neodamodeis* (Thucydides 5.68.1). In addition to these was another *lochos* composed of the men who had fought with Brasidas at Amphipolis, called the *Brasideioi*. Later in Thucydides' account (5.71.3), two of the Spartan *polemarchoi* are named: Hipponoïdas and Aristocles, commanders, positioned on the right in the place of honour.

Thucydides provides a further, extremely useful, breakdown of the Spartan numbers just as the battle got under way (5.68.1–3). Despite his claim that Spartan systems were secretive and that giving exact numbers was impossible, he computes that in each of the seven *lochoi* (including the *Brasideioi*) there were four 'fiftieths' (the *pentekostyes*) and in each of them four *enomotiai*. He further computes that each of these *lochoi* was drawn up in a different depth, as each *lochagos* preferred, but that the average depth was eight ranks. This is an interesting detail since the sources record other phalanx depths – eight (see also Thucydides 4.94.1 & 6.67.1; Xenophon, *Hellenica* 2.4.34), ten (Xenophon, *Hellenica* 2.4.11–12), 12 (Xenophon, *Hellenica* 6.4.12), 16 (Thucydides 6.67.2; Xenophon, *Hellenica* 4.2.18), and even 25 ranks for the Thebans at Delium (Thucydides 4.93.4) – but modern reconstructions usually apply a particular depth across an entire army. If the depth of each individual unit was decided by that unit's commander then this may change how other ancient battles are reconstructed by modern commentators.

Fighting alongside the Spartans were 600 men hailing from Skiris, members of a rural community akin to the *perioeci* from northern Laconia who guarded the road to Tegea. These *Skiritai* were probably light infantry and at Mantinea they would guard the vulnerable left flank of the Spartan phalanx, a position they, and they alone, had the honour of holding (Thucydides 5.67.1).

The seven *lochoi* of the Spartans had a frontage of 448 men (Thucydides 5.68.3). This, in ancient-warfare terms, is rare and dizzying detail. From these numbers it is possible to compute the strength of the Spartans as 3,584 men – 4,184 once the 600 *Skiritai* are added – which would mean that each *lochos* had 512 men, each *pentekostys* had 128 men and each *enomotai* had 32 men. What is more, with an average depth of eight men, each *enomotai* was only four shields across, each *pentekostys* only 16 across and each *lochos* only had a frontage of 64 men. If each man in close formation occupied 1m of space, then the entire Spartan frontage at the battle of Mantinea was less than 500m. Thucydides has already stated (5.60.3 & 5.64.2) that this was the full force of the Spartans.

On the right of the Spartan *lochoi* their allies were drawn up, left to right: the Heraeans from Arcadia, the Maenalians, the Tegeates and a few Spartans (perhaps only a single *enomotia*) on the extreme right of the infantry formation. The right wing was the place of honour, so it was only fitting that a small Spartan unit occupy that position – the Tegeates being next was possibly because the battle was fought close to their city. On the outside of these forces, on each wing, were the Spartan cavalry. The sources do not reveal the numbers of the Heraeans, Maenalians or Tegeates, or of the Spartan cavalry (although they would have been organized into units of fifty, *oulamoi* (Plutarch, *Lycurgus* 23.1). Agis II himself was in the centre of the Spartan line, surrounded by the 300 *hippeis* (Thucydides 5.72.4).

Opposing them were the Mantineans, stationed on the Athenian right wing because the battle was being fought in their territory (Thucydides 5.67.2). Next came the Arcadian allies. No numbers are given for the Mantineans or

This view from Mantinea shows the ruins of the theatre, *c.*370 BC; the flat plain beyond is surrounded by hills. It would have been easy for the forces of the Argive/ Athenian alliance to take a position on a steep hill. It is to the credit of the Spartans – and Agis II – that they were able to lure their enemies down from a commanding position on the high ground to fight on the plain. (DEA/G. DAGLI ORTI/Getty Images)

Arcadians, but it should be noted that that there were Arcadians fighting on both sides. Those on the Spartan side were proving their loyalty (Thucydides 5.57.1) and both sides were engaging in the power politics of Arcadia in the central Peloponnese. Heraea was in western Arcadia close to the border with Elis on the River Alpheius and Maenalia was in south-western Arcadia, near the later Megalopolis although its exact location is debated. The Arcadians on both sides were on the respective right wings of the opposing armies and so did not fight each other in the battle.

Next to the Arcadians came the 1,000 elite Argives. These men were *logades* ('picked'); this term and the word *epilektoi* ('chosen') are used interchangeably for elite units in ancient Greek armies: Diodorus, for instance, calls the same unit of Argives *epilektoi* (12.79.4). These elite Argives were equipped and paid at public expense (Thucydides 5.67.2). Next to them were the remainder of the Argives and beyond them the men of Cleonae and Orneae, other cities of Argolis. Again, the sources give no numbers for these contingents, although earlier Thucydides (5.59.4) mentions the five generals of the Argives, perhaps suggesting a maximum of 5,000 men from Argos, the *pentelochoi*, or 'five companies' (5.72.4). Next to them were the 1,000 Athenians and the 300 *hippeis* were on the extreme left wing. Thucydides states (5.68.1–2) that the Spartan army appeared to be the larger, but that it would be impossible to provide exact numbers. In his frustratingly brief account, Plutarch (*Alcibiades* 15.1) only states that the battle divided the Peloponnese and brought many shields against Sparta.

After setting out his detailed arrangements of the contingents on each side, Thucydides reports (5.69.1) that various exhortations were made among the allied contingents: the Mantineans were reminded that they fought on home soil to defend their freedom, the Argives that they sought to reassert their glory, and the Athenians were enjoined to hold their empire more securely. By contrast, the Spartans sang their traditional war songs to encourage one another (Thucydides 5.69.2; Plutarch, *Customs of the Spartans* 16). These probably included the poetry of Tyrtaeus, which was regarded as useful to enflame the souls of young men (Plutarch, *Sayings of Spartans* 61, *Cleomenes* 2.3 & *Intelligence of Animals* 1.1). Tyrtaeus, of course, encouraged the maintenance of the individual's place in the phalanx and urged the warrior to hold his shield correctly and to close with the enemy (fragments 8 & 11).

The battle commenced (Thucydides 5.70.1) with the Argives and their allies, including the Athenians, advancing enthusiastically and impetuously. This was in contrast to the Spartans, who advanced slowly and to the accompaniment of flutes (*auloi*) as was customary; this accompaniment kept the Spartans in step and in order. Plutarch comments (*Lycurgus* 22.2–3) on the orderliness of Spartan battle – they would make a sacrifice, then the *aulos* players would strike up the hymn to Castor and the Spartans would march in perfect step to the rhythm of the flute (helped by their dance and music training) without a gap in their line.

Now in the Antalya Archaeological Museum, this depiction of a phalanx of hoplites from the Mausoleum of Pericles (the Dynast of Lycia, not the Athenian politician) dates from the early 4th century BC. It shows a variety of helmets and armours used by men in the same phalanx and gives a real sense of a phalanx formation. (Jona Lendering/Wikimedia/CC0)

The grave stele of Dexileos from the Dipylon Cemetery, Keramikos, Athens, dates from 394 BC, after the Peloponnesian War. It shows an Athenian cavalryman riding down an enemy. Neither man wears armour and the shield of the man on the ground is not used in defence. The Athenian cavalry at Mantinea would have operated in such a manner. (Ad Meskens/ Wikimedia/CC BY-SA 4.0)

In the opening stages of the battle it is possible to glimpse the differences between the two societies of Sparta, highly conservative and traditional, and Athens, exuberant and individualistic. As the battle progressed these traits would prove to be an advantage for Sparta and a liability for Athens. In many ways, however, thinking of such divisions overly simplifies ideas about Athens and Sparta; in several aspects of its society, Athens was even more conservative than Sparta and Sparta, in several ways, was remarkably forward-thinking. At Mantinea, however, the simplified picture – conservative Spartans versus exuberant Athenians – held true.

Agis II realized that his left wing was outflanked by the allied right wing, just as his own right wing outflanked the Athenians on the extreme left wing of the allied army. Therefore, the Spartan king despatched the *Skiritai* and the *Brasideioi* to make their line equal to that of the Mantineans and the Arcadians. He also advised two of his *lochoi* – perhaps those of the named *polemarchoi*, Hipponoïdas and Aristocles – to join them. As he gave this order, employing the command structure described by Thucydides, the allies attacked and so the two *polemarchoi* refused to move; they were later accused of cowardice and exiled (Thucydides 5.72.1). Their refusal created a gap in the Spartan line – usually a fatal mistake for a hoplite phalanx in battle. New orders were issued to the *Skiritai* to rejoin the line, but it was too late. When the Mantineans and Arcadians engaged with the *Skiritai* and *Brasideioi*, they routed them, pushing them back to the wagons (Thucydides 5.72.3); the 1,000 elite Argives poured into the gap created in the Spartan line, 'creating havoc' within it.

This should have spelt the end for the Spartans. On the rest of the field, however, they and their allies advanced and fell upon the remainder of the

The armies at Mantinea

Spartan view: The seven Spartan *lochoi* at Mantinea have occupied the left of the line. On the extreme right, a very small contingent of Spartans has been posted (so that the Spartans also occupy the place of honour). In the centre of the Spartan line, King Agis II is stationed, surrounded by his 300 *hippeis*. The rightmost Spartan *lochoi* and the division of the Heraeans next to them face the 1,000 hoplites of Athens, commanded by the *strategos* Laches. The Spartan *lochoi* have sung their traditional war songs and have then advanced almost silently to the accompaniment of the *aulos* flute. The Spartan line, eight ranks deep, advances silently towards their enemy ready to engage and threatening to envelop the enemy left wing – these actions are held off heroically by the Athenian cavalry. The Spartan right and allies are unperturbed by the near-disaster unfolding on their left. There, the remainder of the alliance, the 1,000 picked Argives and the hoplites of Mantinea and Arcadia have exploited a gap in the Spartan line and are pouring through. The Spartans facing the Athenians, however, advance coolly against their enemy. This view depicts the moment just before the lines will engage.

Athenian view: The 1,000-strong Athenian contingent holds the left flank of the allied line. On the extreme left flank are the 300 Athenian cavalry. The Athenians have been drawn up in ten tribal *taxeis*, each approximately 100 men strong. In each *taxis* are approximately three *lochoi*, each with just over 30 men. Each contingent of the allies has heard a speech from their own commanders before advancing noisily toward the enemy, each speech appealing to different desires and virtues. The battle has begun very well for Athens and her allies. With a whooping charge, the allied right wing and the chosen Argives have charged into the *Skiritai* and *Brasideioi* and the gap in the Spartan line, threatening to envelop and destroy the Spartan left flank. The Spartans, however, come on coolly and professionally and, perhaps more disconcerting still, almost silently. This detached professionalism silences the confidence of the allies and, despite the strength of their position and the victory on their own right, they begin to lose confidence. They will, almost as soon as the two lines meet, break and flee, leaving the Athenian contingent and its cavalry to fight a rearguard action and the warriors of the victorious allied right to their own fate.

Argives, the Cleoneans and the Orneates; they also engaged the Athenians. Thucydides relates (5.72.4) that many of the troops of Athens' allies did not wait to come to blows, but gave way as soon as the Spartans advanced. The Athenians too were engaged by the rightmost *lochoi* of the Spartans and probably the men of Herea. Thucydides comments (5.73.1) that the Athenians would have suffered more than any other part of the allied army had it not been for the *hippeis* on their extreme left, who prevented the whole allied line from being surrounded.

The battle was therefore one of two halves. On the Spartan left, Agis II's men were defeated by the Mantineans, Arcadians and elite Argives. On the allied left, the Spartans were victorious against the remainder of the Argives, the Cleoneans and the Orneates. The Athenians alone offered resistance, but they were threatened with being outflanked by the right wing of the Spartans. Agis II, however, realized that his left was in dire straits and so, rather than press on with the victorious part of his line, gave orders that the remainder of the army should assist the left (Thucydides 5.73.2–3). According to Diodorus (12.79.5–6), this is better described as a wheeling to bring the victorious part of the Spartan army against the victorious part of the allied army. This manoeuvre allowed the Athenian troops and their remaining allies to retreat without suffering greater losses. Despite this, however, both Athenian commanders were killed along with 200 other casualties; the Argives, the Cleoneans and the Orneates suffered a total of 700 casualties.

On the Spartan left, the victorious allies of Athens realized that the troops on their own left had been defeated and were fleeing the field. They were therefore disinclined to press their victory further. The Mantineans suffered the worst, while the elite Argives were mostly intact (Thucydides 5.73.3–4). The allied right therefore fled as well. The Mantineans suffered 200 casualties. Their flight was not pursued by the Spartans, who had suffered 300 casualties of their own but who nevertheless raised a victory trophy, stripping the enemy dead. They then collected their own dead and withdrew to Tegea where they buried them. A truce allowed the alliance forces to collect their own slain. The allies of Sparta suffered barely a scratch, implying that the Spartans themselves had done the bulk of the fighting.

Although it is briefer than that of Thucydides, Diodorus' account (12.79.1–7) accords with Thucydides' on the whole; although it differs from it in some details, the differences are not irreconcilable. Diodorus reports (12.79.4) that Mantinea was a sharp battle and that the 1,000 picked (*epilektoi*) Argives were the first to put the Spartans opposite them to flight. This accords with Thucydides' version of events. Then, Diodorus offers a brief summary, stating that the Spartans defeated the enemy troops on the rest of the field before wheeling to turn on the successful Argives. Diodorus offers an alternative version of the final phase of the battle (12.79.6–7), describing the Spartans surrounding the elite Argives and Agis II seeking to destroy them to a man; it would be this act which would wipe out the Spartan king's earlier error. At this moment, however, one of the king's advisors, Pharax, advised him to leave an escape route for the Argives. Diodorus does not use the term *xymboulos*, but it is clear that Pharax is one of the ten *xymbouloi* appointed to oversee the king's activities (Diodorus' version of Agis II's censure is at 12.78.6). The Spartan king had no choice but to obey. In this advice Pharax foresaw the danger inherent in fighting a surrounded enemy who had no chance of escape and so would resist all the harder. Similar advice can be found in other didactic literature (not to mention in Sun Tzu's *Art of War*). Diodorus' account places the battle in 419 BC and locates Alcibiades at the battle, which Thucydides does not, although he states (5.61.2) that Alcibiades was an ambassador at Argos before the battle; not even Plutarch explicitly places him there.

Thucydides' account of the battle of Mantinea is one of the most remarkable in all of ancient history. He comments (5.74.1) that it was the greatest battle that had occurred between Greek states for a very long time and involved the most famous states; not only Athens and Sparta, but Argos too. Not only is the battle description itself clear and precise, but several of Thucydides' comments are the only ones of their kind and are used to inform modern interpretations of all manner of other battles of the hoplite era and beyond. It is while describing the events at Mantinea that Thucydides reveals (5.71.1) that ancient Greek armies would make their right flanks extend beyond their enemy's left wing because of the fear each man had for his uncovered side. This fear meant that each man would shelter his uncovered right side as close to the shield of the man on his right as possible and so as a result, both armies would shift to the right as they advanced. This truism is repeated in modern accounts of nearly every ancient battle to the extent that in some modern reconstructions of hoplite warfare it is rejected as a literary trope – modern 'open' conceptions of the hoplite phalanx simply cannot accommodate the idea of each man sheltering behind the shield of the man to his right. With regard to Mantinea, however, it is not appropriate to dismiss such a claim because the fact that the Argive right wing extended beyond Agis II's left flank is what prompted the Spartan king to station the *Skiritai* and the *Brasideioi* further to the left.

Thucydides' account of Mantinea also provides some of the most detailed surviving information about the numbers and depths of hoplite formations (6.68.3), with an average depth of eight ranks of the Spartans' seven *lochoi*, each with four sub-units of 128 men further subdivided into four. Moreover, the remarkable breakdown of a frontage of 448 men – along with the depth of the formations – gives a total of 4,184 men. This is more detail than is available elsewhere on the make-up of any army until the time of Alexander the Great. The sources usually give large numbers with no breakdown; it is possible to use this information in Thucydides' account to extrapolate the details of earlier, contemporary and even later armies.

Now in the Metropolitan Museum of Art, New York (24.97), this fragment from an Athenian funeral monument, possibly to the war dead, dates from *c.*390 BC, just after the Peloponnesian War. It shows unarmoured hoplites fleeing. Two men wear only tunics (one *exomis* and one *chiton*) and a third is naked. Two of the figures wear *pilos* helmets, but only one has a shield; the other has a cloak and may have discarded his shield. (Metropolitan Museum of Art/Wikimedia/CC0)

Mantinea is also a telling battle because it casts light on the decline in Spartan manpower, the *oliganthropia*, evident during the course of the 5th and 4th centuries BC. At Plataea in 479 BC, Sparta had 5,000 Spartan citizen hoplites (Herodotus 9.28.2), but at Mantinea that number had shrunk to only 4,200: the men of the seven *lochoi*, including the *Brasideioi* and *neodamodeis* and the old and young who had been sent home, so there may have been even fewer, perhaps only 3,600. By the time of the battle of Coronea in 394 BC this had slipped further to 2,500 and by the time of Leuctra in 371 BC, Sparta could field only 1,500 citizen hoplites. It was the one great weakness of the Spartan system: Sparta could not easily or quickly replace lost manpower. At the Battle of Champions in 546 BC (Herodotus 1.82), Sparta had been happy to sacrifice 300 men – but as was apparent at Sphacteria, the threat to much fewer than that number prompted Sparta to sue for peace. It is possible that at some point in Sparta's history a *pentekostys* did actually represent one-fiftieth of the citizen body of 6,400 men, but at no point in the surviving records did Sparta ever have so many. Earlier in the war, prisoner numbers were fewer and they were exchanged man for man (Thucydides 2.103.1–2). At Mantinea, Sparta lost 300 men and it is likely that those losses were hard felt, perhaps prompting some kind of military reform in Sparta.

The issue of elite units at Mantinea is intriguing because the surviving record mentions the picked 1,000 Argives and the actions of the elite 300 Spartan *hippeis* – one of the few times that the latter are named and numbered in the sources; sometimes they are unnamed or given different numbers (or no number) and very often their presence must be assumed or inferred. Thucydides reports (5.72.4) that the Spartan *hippeis* fought around the king; this place for them is affirmed in other sources, but never stated so explicitly. There is also a complicating factor in the nature of the 300 Athenian cavalry. They too are called *hippeis* (cavalry being the literal meaning), but there was an Athenian tradition that Athens too had an elite infantry unit, 300 strong, possibly called the *hippeis*. This unit had fought at Plataea in 479 BC (Herodotus 9.21; Diodorus 11.30.4; Plutarch, *Aristides* 14.3–15.1) and in several battles during the 5th century BC (they might also be mentioned by Aeschines and Andocides, writing about the 450s BC), although they are usually considered to have disappeared before the Peloponnesian War. Pausanias (1.27.1) also mentions them at Plataea, but makes them cavalry.

At Mantinea, the actions of only 300 Athenian *hippeis* on the extreme left holding off the advance and envelopment of the Spartans and their allies seems unlikely for cavalry; that was not the role of mounted troops at the

Now in the National Archaeological Museum, Athens (3708), this depiction of an Athenian cavalryman dates from *c*.400 BC, just after the Peloponnesian War. He wears a cloak and *chiton* plus a *petasos* hat, originally from Thessaly and common rural attire throughout ancient Greece. His opponent wears an *exomis* and has a more elaborate helmet – perhaps Chalkidian, although without cheek pieces – and he carries a shield which seems to have notches cut out of it, in the style of a Boeotian shield (a type of which no trace has been found archaeologically, but which is common in sculpture and on coins, especially from Thebes). (George E. Koronaios/ Wikimedia/CC BY-SA 4.0)

These hoplites and archers from the Nereid Monument carry a variety of equipment. One man's shield has a shield curtain, a detail not apparent in contemporary art throughout the Peloponnesian War. (Prisma/Universal Images Group via Getty Images)

time: usually they were used for scouting or running down fleeing foes. It is therefore possible that these 300 Athenian *hippeis* were an elite unit of infantry of long standing. It is also possible that this force was the 300 men despatched as a garrison to Epidaurus (Thucydides 5.56.1). In that reference they are not called *hippeis*; nor are they labelled elite in any way, although their commander is named, Agesippidas, and the commander of the elite Athenian unit was named stretching back to Plataea. Such a suggestion would, however, rewrite the history of Athenian infantry actions and it is probably best to consider these 300 *hippeis* as cavalry. Diodorus states that there were only 200 cavalry, which removes the identification with an elite infantry unit entirely – but he also states that the force of 1,000 Athenians was picked and therefore elite. Diodorus may have conflated the evidence. If this was a force of only 200 cavalry, however, it makes their heroic actions on the left flank of the Athenian and allied line all the more remarkable.

Plutarch offers a valuable insight (*Alcibiades* 15.1) in commenting that the battle was fought so far from Athens that Sparta's victory brought it no great advantage over Athens whereas, if the Spartans had lost, Sparta's very existence would have been threatened. In that regard, the battle was a very close-run thing. Agis II cannot have intended to create a dangerous gap in his line through which the elite Argives rushed. The reliability and calm resolve of the rest of the Spartan king's troops who defeated the remaining alliance troops and then turned and dealt with the elite Argives was a phenomenal vote of confidence in the abilities and reliability of the Spartan *lochoi* – especially when the Spartan left had been defeated. Had the Spartans broken and fled as the Mantineans and Athenians did, the day, and perhaps Sparta itself, would have been lost. Thucydides' summary (5.72.2–3) is insightful: the Spartans proved inferior in tactical skill, but showed that they were superior in courage. If the remainder of the allied forces, including the Athenians, could have held their line for longer, the elite Argives may have turned the battle in their favour and the entire Peloponnesian War would have taken a very different course.

Analysis

ATHENIAN EFFECTIVENESS

Athens could call upon many more hoplites than Sparta could, but chose to avoid head-on confrontation. Even when Athenian forces had a numerical advantage over the Spartans, such as on Sphacteria, the Athenian hoplites relied upon lightly armed troops to inflict damage on the enemy before they closed in. Perhaps the quality of Athenian hoplites was questionable: at Amphipolis a force of only 150 Spartans was able to rout a force which outnumbered them by perhaps 4 to 1, and at Mantinea the Athenians broke and ran with their allies. On other occasions – and usually against non-Spartan enemies – Athenian hoplites did perform better (although not always, as Delium showed).

Athens began the war with a clear strategy which acknowledged that its strengths lay in the Athenian navy. If the Athenians could avoid large-scale conflicts with Spartan armies and instead raid the coasts of their enemies,

The Pnyx, a hill in Athens, was where the assembly (*ekklesia*) would meet. It was here that the expeditions of the Athenians were proposed and voted on. Speakers would address the gathered citizens from the platform (*bema*) in the centre. Although the remains date from a later era, the space and layout were the same during the Peloponnesian War. (George E. Koronaios/Wikimedia/ CC BY-SA 4.0)

Like Eupolis, Aristophanes found fault with the Athenian commanders of the Peloponnesian War and sought to hold them to account in his plays. Aristophanes especially targeted Cleon in several plays until Cleon's death at Amphipolis in 422 BC. He is the only author of the 'Old Comedy' (from about 60 known authors) whose plays survive. Unlike Eupolis, Aristophanes lived on beyond the war, dying in c.386 BC. (DeAgostini/Getty Images)

they could incrementally undermine Sparta's ability and willingness to fight on. Athens had more men, money and resources than Sparta, but still Pericles realized that facing Sparta's hoplites en masse could spell the end. In the early part of the war, as the battle of Naupactus showed, the Athenian navy could literally run rings around the Spartan and Corinthian opposition. It would take years, and a second insightful Spartan (after Brasidas) in Lysander – not to mention Persian funds – for Sparta to develop a fleet that could compete. Even with the ravages of the plague, Athens could have continued with this policy until Sparta wearied of the war or suffered a major mishap (as would occur at Sphacteria).

Pericles' death robbed Athens of its guiding hand, however, and he was replaced by a series of ambitious, opportunistic and selfish politicians who looked to their own glory before the benefit of Athens, although they would have argued that those things were one and the same. Such men had existed under Pericles, but they had been held in check. With his death, and therefore unchecked, they ran riot. Some proved themselves good commanders in the field, while others were disastrous. Demosthenes was remarkably successful at Sphacteria, but it was an unexpected victory and one which showed the best results of Athenian ambition, opportunism and selfish glory-seeking. It was at Sphacteria that Athens' hoplites – not to mention all its troops, down to the humblest *psilos* – proved their mettle and demonstrated that, given the right circumstances, they could be a match for Sparta's vaunted land forces. The Athenians also gained immensely in confidence. Earlier, however, after defeat in Aetolia, Demosthenes had been unwilling to return to Athens for fear of what the city would do to him because he had failed. He redeemed his reputation at Olpae.

The ups and downs of the careers of Athens' generals also show one of Athens' weaknesses – working for a fickle electorate which could easily be swayed by political enemies who simply wanted their own selfish chance of glory. This was evident in the career of Cleon – he was forced to take command before Sphacteria not because he was expected to succeed, but the opposite. Cleon's disastrous campaign towards Amphipolis started well with the bold seizure of Torone, but the panic and shambles outside Amphipolis meant Athens had to sue for peace. Amphipolis, however, was necessary – Athens could not allow a rampant Brasidas to take away cities in the region which provided Athens with timber and grain. Weakened by plague and defeat, Athens had only 6,000 adult male hoplites left, but the threat posed by Brasidas' seizure of Amphipolis meant it was well worth mounting an expedition composed of one-fifth of Athens' total remaining hoplites.

Before Amphipolis, however, the Athenians had revealed another inherent problem – hubris. No matter the quality of its hoplites or its fleet, Athens was undermined by the selfish and short-sighted ambitions of its leading politicians. After Sphacteria, Athens (led by Cleon) arrogantly refused peace overtures from Sparta. Even though Sparta was hamstrung and did not invade the following year, or take any aggressive action, Athens squandered its advantages with an ambitious and over-reaching campaign to seize territory in Boeotia. The defeat at Delium cost Athens dearly, sacrificing 15 per cent of its available manpower (not to mention empowering an old enemy in Thebes).

Athens was therefore forced to sue for peace after Amphipolis, not from a position of strength but from a position of equal weakness.

Athenian involvement in Mantinea represented another squandering of the advantage. Athenian forces should have been recuperating, but lost another 200 hoplites – by then perhaps almost 5 per cent of Athens' manpower. Worse was to come, revealing that Athens did not – perhaps could not – learn from its mistakes. On Sicily and subsequently, Athens' overconfidence cost it dearly. In 406 BC Athens won the naval battle of Arginusae, but then voted to put all the Athenian admirals to death because the crews of 25 triremes – 5,000 men – could not be saved (Xenophon, *Hellenica* 1.6.1–34). Time and time again Athens squandered its advantages by favouring the selfish justifications of its leading men.

SPARTAN EFFECTIVENESS

The Spartans and their allies had a fearsome reputation as the best hoplites in Greece. The entire Spartan system was geared to creating the best hoplites, and therefore the best citizens. Throughout the war, Spartan armies were repeatedly avoided by their Athenian counterparts. In a way this was proof of their reputation.

On the battlefield, however, when conflict was inevitable, it is evident that the Spartan hoplites had mixed results. At Mantinea they certainly proved to be disciplined and better fighters than most of the men ranged against them, although the elite Argives were a match for them. The remarkable discipline of the victorious Spartan right was shown in the ability to halt while pushing the Athenians and their allies back, redress their line and turn to the left in order to assist their beleaguered left wing. At Olpae, however, where the Spartan contingent was ambushed and routed, the Peloponnesian allies broke quickly and fled, so the victory of Spartan armies was far from assured. At Amphipolis, a very small number of Spartan hoplites were able to wreak havoc on the numerically superior Athenian line. Surely if the Athenians had dressed their line and turned to face the Spartan charge, the men of Athens could have emerged victorious, given the advantages bestowed by occupying the high ground and superiority of numbers.

In many ways, however, Brasidas' boldness was the antithesis of the Spartan way of war. At Sphacteria, despite being so massively outnumbered, the 420 hoplites sought to engage the enemy in the usual way – a frontal charge on the Athenian hoplites, who outnumbered them 2 to 1. Even before Sphacteria, the Athenian forces had gained confidence during their defence of Pylos in which, assaulting walls, the Spartans were less effective. At Sphacteria, the Spartans were then frustrated and held in check by the vast numbers of missile troops, including those throwing rocks, that the Athenians could bring to bear, but the men of Sparta did not try to attempt any kind of tactical innovation (Demosthenes had feared they would). At Mantinea, the Spartans affected just such a frontal charge against enemy hoplites, confident that the enemy would waver, which they did. Sphacteria witnessed the growing confidence of humble *psiloi* once they realized that even they could hold Spartan hoplites at bay.

It is clear that the Spartans were highly effective hoplites and their purposeful discipline is commented on more than once (and contrasted with the unruly shouting of their enemies). When required to innovate, however, many Spartan commanders seem to have been stymied – they did a set number of things very well, but when required to think more creatively, they simply did the same things, relying on discipline, professionalism and reputation. It was Brasidas who did things differently, and the sources make it clear that many at Sparta were jealous of him or saw him as an upstart. Nevertheless, several rebels went to join him, especially when Sparta had become timid after the defeat at Sphacteria.

The defeat at Sphacteria highlights the greatest weakness in Spartan effectiveness: manpower. Spartan armies could be defeated and yet Sparta's reputation as the pre-eminent producer of hoplites remained remarkably intact because those who survived stayed true to the values of the *agoge* system. As Sphacteria showed, however, Sparta simply could not afford such losses in manpower. A system which required boys from the age of seven to keep training until they were 60 could not be replenished easily. The potential loss of only 120 hoplites at Sphacteria (even if they were the most important men) should not have been a crippling blow for Sparta, but it was. In the other battles fought, Spartan losses were relatively low – 50 at Sphacteria, 300 at Mantinea, and reportedly only seven at Amphipolis! – but cumulatively, those losses crippled Sparta. The long-term ramifications of those losses would not be realized for another 40 years, and the confidence other Greek communities should have gained in the defeats they could inflict upon the Spartans and Sparta's growing weaknesses would take some time to be realized as well. Perhaps Sparta's greatest assets, and the reasons the Spartans would eventually emerge triumphant in the Peloponnesian War, were not its own qualities and reputation but the fatal flaws in its opponent.

Aftermath

Athens did not suffer after the defeat at Mantinea, but seemed almost to compound its squandering of the peace by launching an ambitious, unnecessary and aggressive plan to attack Sicily and bring it into the Athenian empire. These Athenian actions also allowed the war to be fought indirectly, with the Spartans joining on the side of Syracuse. The Sicilian expedition of 415 BC ended in utter disaster for Athens in 413 BC when the entire Athenian force was destroyed, losing almost 200 ships (with 40,000 rowers) and 5,000 citizen hoplites; there were probably almost 50,000 men of allied forces who also perished. The war was renewed in 413 BC – the 50-year peace had lasted barely eight years.

The Spartans now did something different that altered the course and outcome of the war. Throughout the Archidamian War, Spartan forces had invaded Attica and ravaged the land only to return to Sparta for the winter. Now, in 413 BC, they captured the town of Decelea, only a short distance from Athens – visible from its walls, in fact – and there they stayed. This meant they could prevent the Athenians from leaving the city and allowed the Spartans to launch raids into Attica throughout the year. The defeat on Sicily also damaged Athens' reputation and its ability to control its empire. Allies all over the Athenian empire began to revolt and Athens was thrown into political turmoil. The Democracy was briefly overthrown in 411 BC by an oligarchy but, in a sign of Athens' tremendous resilience, the Athenians fought on, rebuilt their army and navy and even won several victories, such as at Arginusae in 406 BC.

The setbacks suffered by Athens in the Sicilian expedition and subsequently had two major ramifications. First, the war shifted into the Aegean Sea – Athens' back yard – just as Athens' allies deserted it and Athens' navy (and financial resources) shrank. This allowed Sparta and its allies to build up their own naval resources and vie with Athens on an even footing. The second ramification was that Persia, defeated 50 years earlier and kept

This double-headed portrait bust of the historians Herodotus (left) and Thucydides (right) is now in the National Archaeological Museum, Naples (Inv. 6239). Herodotus lived into the era of the Peloponnesian War and Thucydides set up his own 'scientific' history of that conflict in opposition to the more fable-based history of the Greco-Persian Wars produced by Herodotus. (Bettmann/Getty Images)

An Athenian funerary *loutrophoros* now in the National Archaeological Museum, Athens. Dating to just after the Peloponnesian War, it shows a slave carrying the shield and helmet of his master. The master wears a sword and a bronze 'muscled' cuirass, suggesting that this equipment could still be used at that time. The Phrygian helmet is also unusual and is usually associated with the later 4th century BC, but its presence suggests that different styles were used. The roles of slaves are absent in the sources; helots are occasionally mentioned for Spartan forces. If such slaves fought, they would have fought as *psiloi*, throwing rocks or whatever came to hand. (Marsyas/Wikimedia/CC BY 2.5)

out of the Aegean by the growth and power of the Delian League, now saw an opportunity to wield power and influence in the region once again. Persia's leadership – especially Tissaphernes, the satrap of Lydia – provided support and ships for those former allies of Athens which broke away and, when approached by the Spartan general Lysander, money for a Spartan fleet. As already noted, Persian envoys had travelled to Sparta as early as 425 BC. Lysander's foresight in developing a Spartan navy sealed Athens' fate. In 405 BC the Athenian fleet was destroyed at Aegospotami and Athens no longer had the financial resources to build another. That victory also allowed Sparta to cut off Athens' supply of grain from the Black Sea and essentially starve Athens into submission.

Still Athens tried to fight on, but in 404 BC it surrendered unconditionally. Athens' walls were torn down as part of the terms of surrender, a Spartan garrison was installed and Athens' democracy was replaced with a government of Thirty Tyrants who were pro-Spartan and who punished Athenian citizens, eliminating opposition and any who might show potential to oppose Spartan will. The Spartan victory in the Peloponnesian War was the zenith of Sparta's power and dominance of Greece, and yet the reassertion of Persian influence was an ominous sign of things to come. The continuing ambition, resilience and confidence of Athens and other Greek city-states would mean that the end of Sparta's power was within sight.

BIBLIOGRAPHY

Ancient sources

Historians can draw upon several sources for the Peloponnesian War from a wide variety of genres ranging from archaeology and art through to literature of every kind. The most important of these are the historians **Thucydides**, an Athenian aristocratic general who wrote a history of the war covering the events of 431–410 BC and is regarded as the first 'scientific' historian, and **Xenophon**, who wrote a continuation of Thucydides' work (the *Hellenica*), covering the end of the war and continuing to 362 BC. Thucydides was exiled from Athens following the debacle at Amphipolis and, even though Xenophon was an Athenian, he was an admirer of Sparta and so the perspectives of these two works are markedly different. Thucydides prided himself on his neutrality and even-handedness and his work is still regarded as one of the best examples of ancient-history writing.

There are other surviving sources too, from historians such as **Diodorus Siculus**, who culled other sources to write his own *Universal History* in the 1st century BC. Often, Diodorus preserves works and opinions which are otherwise lost (and which offer different perspectives from Thucydides and Xenophon). Other later writers, such as **Plutarch**, writing in the early 2nd century AD, record much which is precious – both in his *Lives* and his wide-ranging *Moralia* (or *Moral Essays*) which includes many anecdotes, on Spartan life especially. Plutarch was not a historian, more a moral biographer and essayist, but often military historians must use his works for their historical material because it is not preserved anywhere else. There are also works from much later, even down to the Byzantine age, which saw the compilation of all sorts of sources (many of which are otherwise lost). The kernels that can be gleaned from the works of writers such as **Athenaeus** and **Suidas**, the author of the *Suda*, are often priceless.

Also available are diverse types of literature, from the plays of **Aristophanes** and the dialogues of **Plato** to the speeches of Athenian orators who employed historical anecdotes to show how learned they were about Athens' past. The political and philosophical writings of **Aristotle** are also useful but often they merge a vast swathe of history into a single snapshot which combines multiple periods. Added to these, there is a vast store of anecdotal information in sources such as the stratagem collections of **Polyaenus of Macedon** and **Sextus Julius Frontinus**, the *Varia Historia* of **Aelian** (not the *Tactica* author but writing in the early 3rd century AD), the *Attic Nights* of **Aulus Gellius** and the *Facta et Dicta Memorabilia* of **Valerius Maximus**. Although most were written centuries later, they often preserve information (or versions of events) not found in surviving narratives. Some of Plutarch's essays in the *Moralia* also belong to this tradition. These works also preserve a genre of apothegms (sayings) of many of the protagonists involved. Many of these sources must be used with great care, but doing so can reveal a great deal about what happened during the Peloponnesian War. In many cases, these sources provide a much more nuanced and detailed story of what was going on, especially in Athens, during the war or they corroborate a picture suggested by the main historians. For instance, it is from a single fragment of a play by **Eupolis** that historians have learned that the Spartans used the lambda on their shields. Eupolis wrote all of his plays during wartime, between 429 and 411 BC. Eupolis served in the Athenian navy as a rower, and possibly as a hoplite early in the conflict. **Socrates'** position in his own trial suggests that the later ephebic oath existed before the Peloponnesian War. Indeed, the Socratic dialogues, nearly all of which are set during the war, offer all sorts of military insights.

In addition to these written sources there is also the rich archaeological record, with especially valuable details of arms and equipment – and even burial trends – revealed by funerary sculpture and pottery. Often this kind of evidence tells a story which literature does not. Analysis of contemporary pottery, for instance, suggests that greaves fell out of use *c.*460 BC and that the cloak became an important symbol of service – it may also have been used as a defensive (or even offensive) device. The cheaper *pilos* helmet also became more common. Several inscriptions offer corroboration of the written histories or add detail to them (and sometimes they contradict them). The geography of Greece itself is also a wonderful resource – a place like Sphacteria has remained remote, perhaps largely unchanged, since 425 BC and the island still tells the story of that battle. In many other places in Greece the landscape is still largely as it was.

Classical works

Aelian, trans. A.M. Devine (1980). *Tactica*, in 'Aelian's Manual of Hellenistic Military Tactics. A New Translation from the Greek with an Introduction', *The Ancient World* 19: 31–64.

Aeschines, trans. C.D. Adams (1919). Cambridge, MA & London: Harvard University Press.

Andocides, trans. K.J. Maidment & J.O. Burtt (1941). *Minor Attic Orators*, Vol. 1. Cambridge, MA & London: Harvard University Press.

Aristophanes, trans. J. Henderson (1998–2007). 5 volumes (*Clouds, Wasps, Knights, Lysistrata, Acharnians*). Cambridge, MA & London: Harvard University Press.

Aristotle, trans. H. Rackham (1935). 21 volumes (Vol. 20, *Athenian Constitution*). Cambridge, MA & London: Harvard University Press.

Diodorus Siculus, trans. C.H. Oldfather (1946). 12 volumes (Vol. 4, books IX–XII.40). Cambridge, MA & London: Harvard University Press.

Diodorus Siculus, trans. C.H. Oldfather (1950). 12 volumes (Vol. 5, books XII.41–XIII). Cambridge, MA & London: Harvard University Press.

Eupolis, trans. I.C. Storey (2011). *Fragments of Old Comedy*, Vol. 2. Cambridge, MA & London: Harvard University Press.

Frontinus, trans. C.E. Bennett (1925). *The Stratagems*. Cambridge, MA & London: Harvard University Press.

Lycurgus, trans. K.J. Maidment & J.O. Burtt (1954). *Minor Attic Orators*, Vol. 2. Cambridge, MA & London: Harvard University Press.

Lysias, trans. W.R.M. Lamb (1930). Cambridge, MA & London: Harvard University Press.

Pausanias, trans. W.H.S. Jones (1918–55). *Description of Greece*. 5 volumes. Cambridge, MA & London: Harvard University Press.

Plato, trans. H.N. Fowler (1914). 12 volumes (Vol. 1, *Apology*). Cambridge, MA & London: Harvard University Press.

Plato, trans. W.R.M. Lamb (1925). 12 volumes (Vol. 3, *Symposium*). Cambridge, MA & London: Harvard University Press.

Plato, trans. R.G. Bury (1926). 12 volumes (Vol. 9, *Laws*). Cambridge, MA & London: Harvard University Press.

Plutarch, trans. B. Perrin (1916). *Plutarch's Lives* in 11 volumes (Vol. 3, *Life of Pericles*). Cambridge, MA & London: Harvard University Press.

Plutarch, trans. B. Perrin (1916). *Plutarch's Lives* in 11 volumes (Vol. 4, *Life of Alcibiades*). Cambridge, MA & London: Harvard University Press.

Plutarch, trans. F.C. Babbitt (1931). *Plutarch's Moralia* in 16 volumes (Vol. 3, *Sayings of Spartans, Spartan Customs, Sayings of Spartan Women*). Cambridge, MA & London: Harvard University Press.

Polyaenus, trans. P. Krentz & E.L. Wheeler (1994). *Stratagems of War*. 2 volumes. Chicago, IL: Ares.

Polybius, trans. W.R. Paton (1922–26). *The Histories*. 6 volumes. Cambridge, MA & London: Harvard University Press.

Strabo, trans. H.L. Jones (1917–32). *The Geography*. 8 volumes. Cambridge, MA & London: Harvard University Press.

Thucydides, trans. C.F. Smith (1919–23). 4 volumes. Cambridge, MA & London: Harvard University Press.

Tyrtaeus, trans. D.E. Gerber (1999), in *Greek Elegiac Poetry*. Cambridge, MA & London: Harvard University Press.

Xenophon, trans. C.L. Brownson (1918–21). *Hellenica*. 2 volumes. Cambridge, MA & London: Harvard University Press.

Xenophon, trans. E.C. Marchant (1923). *Memorabilia, Oeconomicus, Symposium, & Apology*. Cambridge, MA & London: Harvard University Press.

Xenophon, trans. E.C. Marchant (1925). *Scripta Minora (Spartan Constitution)*. Cambridge, MA & London: Harvard University Press.

Modern works

Cartledge, P. (2002). *The Spartans. An Epic History*. London: Macmillan.

Crowley, J. (2012). *The Psychology of the Athenian Hoplite: The Culture of Combat in Classical Athens*. Cambridge: Cambridge University Press.

de Ste Croix, G.E.M. (1972). *The Origins of the Peloponnesian War*. London: Duckworth.

Figueira, T.J. (1986). 'Population patterns in Sparta' *Transactions of the American Philological Association* 116: 165–213.

Forrest, W.G. (1968). *A History of Sparta 950–192 BC.* London: Hutchinson & Co.

Hanson, V.D. (2005). *A War Like No Other.* New York, NY: Random House.

Hodkinson, S. & Powell, A., eds (2006). *Sparta & War.* Swansea: The Classical Press of Wales.

Hornblower, S. (1991). *A Commentary of Thucydides: Volume I: Books I–III.* Oxford: Clarendon Press.

Hornblower, S. (1996). *A Commentary of Thucydides: Volume II: Books IV–V.24.* Oxford: Clarendon Press.

Hornblower, S. (2008). *A Commentary of Thucydides: Volume III: Books 5.25–8.109.* Oxford: Oxford University Press.

Jones, N. (1977). 'The Topography and Strategy of the Battle of Amphipolis in 422 B.C.', *California Studies in Classical Antiquity* 10: 71–104.

Kagan, D. (1969). *The Outbreak of the Peloponnesian War.* Ithaca, NY: Cornell University Press.

Kagan, D. (1974). *The Archidamian War.* Ithaca, NY: Cornell University Press.

Kagan, D. (1981). *The Peace of Nicias and the Sicilian Expedition.* Ithaca, NY: Cornell University Press.

Kagan, D. (1987). *The Fall of the Athenian Empire.* Ithaca, NY: Cornell University Press.

Kagan, D. (2003). *The Peloponnesian War.* London: Viking Penguin.

Kagan, D. (2010). *Thucydides: The Reinvention of History.* Harmondsworth: Penguin Books.

Kagan, D. & Viggiano, G.F., eds (2013). *Men of Bronze: Hoplite Warfare in Ancient Greece.* Princeton, NJ: Princeton University Press.

Lazenby, J.F. (1985). *The Spartan Army.* Oxford: Aris & Phillips.

Palagia, O. (2009). *Art in Athens during the Peloponnesian War.* Cambridge: Cambridge University Press.

Powell, A. (1988). *Athens and Sparta: Constructing Greek Political and Social History from 478 B.C.* London: Routledge.

Rhodes, P.J. & Osborne, R., eds & trans. (2003). *Greek Historical Inscriptions 404–323 BC.* Oxford: Oxford University Press.

Roberts, M. (2015). *Two Deaths at Amphipolis: Cleon vs Brasidas in the Peloponnesian War.* Barnsley: Pen & Sword Military.

Rood, T. (2004). *Thucydides: Narrative and Explanation.* Oxford: Oxford University Press.

Snodgrass, A.M. (1967). *Arms and Armour of the Greeks.* Ithaca, NY: Cornell University Press.

These hoplites on the Nereid Monument show a variety of equipment. The armour appears to have been simplified, although details could have been painted on originally. There is evidence of an archer at left, and two men employing overhand spear-throwing postures. (Universal History Archive/ Universal Images Group via Getty Images)

INDEX

References to illustrations are shown in **bold**. References to plates are shown in bold with caption pages in brackets, e.g. **52–53**, (54).